Contents

Publisher's Note

This interview, conducted by Catherine Bernstein, took place on May 5, 2006, as part of *Memories of the Shoah*, a collection initiated by the Foundation for the Memory of the Shoah and the National Audiovisual Institute. In fall 2024, Roman Polanski agreed to turn this oral testimony into a written text, which he reviewed and corrected in its entirety.

Introduction

I have already spoken on several occasions about those times. At the end of the 1970s, for the autobiography I was about to write, I gathered my thoughts and put my memories in order for the first time. I treated the events described in that book subjectively, striving above all to depict faithfully the experience of a little boy who has been hurled into a nightmare beyond his understanding and that he was seeking to resist in his own childish way in order to survive.

I was six years and thirteen days old when the War broke out, and twelve when it ended. The greatest suffering I experienced at that time wasn't due to material conditions—misery or hunger—or even to fear. It was caused by my parents' absence and my heartrending longing to see them again, my isolated existence in a world turned strange and cold.

I had to confront those memories again at the request of Steven Spielberg and his Shoah Foundation, founded in 1994 as an archive of testimonies from Holocaust survivors, which today number in the tens of thousands. In this new context, I had to re-examine everything that had happened to me from a broader perspective, as part of a phenomenon that seemed inconceivable and was, undoubtedly, unique in human history: a handful of psychopaths' systematic attempt at the complete extermination of the Jewish people.

In 2005, L'Institut national de l'audiovisuel[1] (INA), in collaboration with the French Foundation for the Memory of the Shoah, launched a similar ambitious project, aiming to preserve the memories of the last survivors in audiovisual form. My interview is among the hundred or so conducted as part of this project.

The book we are presenting to readers today is based on this several-hours-long recording.

I must admit that when I agreed to the publication of this interview in this new form, I hadn't imagined how much work transcribing such a conversation would require. By nature, it's full of digressions, unfinished sentences, and interrupted threads. However, from the very start, I insisted we not smooth out or round off this original narrative too much. I hope we've managed to find the necessary balance, which is largely thanks to our editor, Sandrine Treiner.

As it has turned out, the text we're placing in readers' hands seems more like a sketch, filtered and restored to its essentials. Let this be my final word on the matter. Memory will bring me nothing new; on the contrary, it risks taking something away.

The two documents in this book that constitute my father's memories were written earlier and have their own history.

1 Translator's Note: National Institute for the Audiovisual.

The first, "My Path to Mauthausen," is a letter he sent me in 1973 after a ridiculous argument we had over the telephone. The War had torn us apart. The years of separation had tortured us in very different, but equally cruel, ways, and we'd both found ourselves profoundly changed. But this was particularly striking in the barely adolescent boy I was at the time.

We never spoke about these experiences. Years later, it would be discovered that such silence was common. It has now been documented and studied with the subtlest tools of modern psychology. But from our perspective, it was infinitely simpler (I believe I can also speak for my father). To put it bluntly, the subject pissed us off! We had no desire to discuss it. There were so many more interesting and important things, such as life and the future.

And so, thirty years after his return from Hell, and with me in mind for the first time, my father described the most horrible period of his life.

I then asked him to broaden the subject by recounting everything that had preceded the Mauthausen camp, as well as what he'd experienced immediately after the War.

I received his manuscript in autumn 1975. Busy filming *The Tenant*, I put it in a drawer and—shame on me—forgot about it.

It was only the work on the Flammarion publishing project,[2]

---

2 Translator's Note: The author is referring to this book you are reading, which was published in French by Flammarion under the title "*Ne courez pas ! Marchez ! suivi de Lettres à mon fils de Ryszard Polanski. Lettres traduites du polonais et annotée par Piotr Kaminski.*" The book consists of Polanski's interview about his wartime experiences for the INA and the Foundation for the Memory of

fifty years later, that reminded me of it. I found it brilliantly written, in a very original tone, and, after some necessary checks and cuts, entirely worthy of publication.

Especially today, when, once again, you feel like shouting with Ferdinand in Shakespeare's *The Tempest*, "Hell is empty; all the devils are here!"

---

the Shoah, as well as letters from his father, translated from the Polish.

Don't Run! Walk!

As you've requested, I've brought you a few photographs. There aren't many, of course, because most documents like that didn't survive the War. But there were some with members of my family or other people.

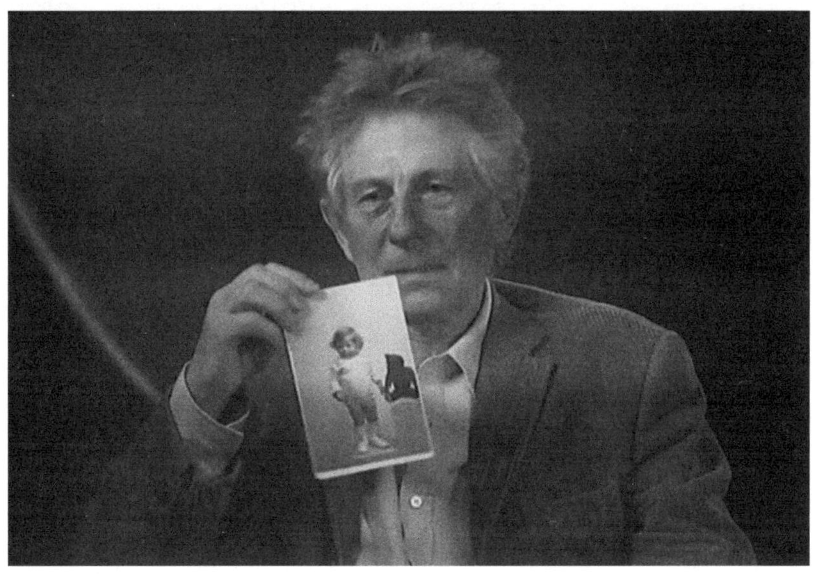

I'll start with my oldest photograph, in which I'm barely three years old.

It was taken in Paris, where I was born. My parents lived there.

I don't know why they chose Paris to live. They undoubtedly had the aspirations of people coming to France at that time—meaning that they didn't arrive like today's immigrants, who are often hostile to the local culture. On the contrary, they admired France's institutions, history, ethics.

When I was born, they'd already been there for a few years.

This photo, taken after our return to Kraków in 1936, shows my father, his two brothers, and my mother. I'm about three years old. Why did they leave France? I've been aware that such a question would be asked. I think they had financial difficulties and were homesick.

Here, I'm around five or six years old.

My parents weren't very observant. Not at all, in fact.

My father had worked in several professions. For a long time, he was a sales representative. He worked for a record company, or rather, at a store that belonged to a record company: His Master's Voice. Everybody is familiar with the logo of that company: a dog listening to a gramophone.

After leaving France, we returned to Poland—Kraków, specifically. My earliest childhood memories begin there.

I remember very well the apartment we lived in when I was three and a half or four. It had balcony overlooking a large, empty space—that part of Kraków hadn't been very built up yet. There was, on the other hand, a market right in front of our building.

Opposite our building and across the street was another. Today, that part of the city is completely urbanized, but back then it was more like a suburb. And I do remember our neighbors, even the names of the two boys who lived on the same floor as us. I lived there with my parents and my sister. Our place was small, but it smelled new. It was a new building.

Our building had four or five floors, with two apartments per floor. We lived on the third. Our neighbors were the Kostrzewas. One of the two boys was called Titek—I don't know what his real first name was. Our home was peaceful.

We had no servants, except for a young cleaning woman who came occasionally, at least for a while, but not for the entire time we lived there.

Socially, my parents were middle class.

When I arrived in Poland, I could already speak Polish, which, along with French, was my native language. However, I rolled my 'r's in the French way, which made everyone laugh.

For quite a long time, probably until I was six or seven, I couldn't pronounce the '*r*' the Polish way.

My parents knew Yiddish but didn't speak it at all in their daily lives. It was only later, when I found myself in the ghetto, that I had a little more of a chance to hear Yiddish spoken. There were, of course, all kinds of Jews in Poland. Most of the Jews you encountered on a day-to-day basis had descended from different waves of immigration but were fully integrated. Most had been there for six to eight centuries.

My parents had non-Jewish friends, as did I. The friends who lived on our floor, for example, were Gentile.

The entire family participated in two or three of the important religious holidays, such as the Seder at Passover. In general, these were occasions for the whole family to gather around the same table; but apart from that, my parents didn't practice religion. I had an uncle who took me to synagogue two or three times so I could see what it was like and learn about certain rites. But since I was a child, I of course wasn't at all interested. I was rather bored, in fact. I wasn't a believer.

Moreover, when we talk about what happened, we should leave aside the question of whether the victims were believers or not. Whether they were religious or not changed absolutely nothing. Nor did it change what happened to us, either.

Poland had few opportunities for entertainment when I was very young. There was one, however, that I never missed. I'm referring to a celebration that still exists in Kraków and is called *Wianki*. This ancient pagan tradition is still being practiced on the Vistula, the Polish river that flows past Wawel, the enormous royal castle in Kraków. It's the kind of festival presented each summer on a single evening. I can't remember whether that is in July or August.[3] I think that what's being celebrated is about a Polish princess who refused to marry a German, preferring to throw herself into the river. There are barges that float on the Vistula and performances that take place on the water. Featured are wreaths of flowers with lights and candles in memory, or to the glory, of this princess.

Wianki is the plural of *Wianek*, which means *wreath* in Polish and from which the event derives its name. In Poland, girls used to wear wreaths of flowers. The celebration always ends with a big fireworks display. The entire population of Kraków gathers on the hillside and on top of the walls of the great castle to watch the show.[4] And there were lots of people back then. It was a big celebration for children that we found unforgettable. We looked forward to that day eagerly.

The Threat and the War

I, of course, have a wealth of memories linked to the beginning of the War, and even from before it broke out, because there was a very distinctive pre-war atmosphere. I was only six years old when it started. Before it, there were rumors circulating. People began to be afraid long before the German invasion. It wasn't a surprise since we were expecting something. Hitler had been right at the border for three years. We could see what was happening, how it was shaping up. At first, you couldn't take him too seriously, in the same way, for example, that we

3 Translator's Note: Traditionally, the festival takes place during the summer solstice, around the 21st and 22nd of June.

4 Kraków was the capital of Poland from 1038 to 1596, before King Zygmunt III Vasa moved the royal residence to Warsaw in 1596.

aren't taking what is happening in Iran seriously enough at the current time. The threats from their supreme leader aren't worrying us as much as they should. Hitler's threats also seemed absurd. When he harangued the German crowds with shouts, he could even seem quite comic, but he also hypnotized his audience. And then things started to become increasingly serious until people talked of nothing else.

There is one moment I remember particularly: I was walking with my father in Planty Park, the one in Kraków that had replaced the old ramparts and surrounded the city. There was a guy with a little table selling drawings. Quite a few people had gathered around him and were watching. He talked a lot and showed what he was doing with the drawings, which depicted four German leaders: Goering, Goebbels, Hitler (I think) and . . . Himmler, probably. Folding the paper in a certain way turned the drawing into a pig. My father explained to me why the guy had designed this pig and who those people were. That was my first notion of the threat.

Just before the War broke out, we moved. We went to live at my grandmother's because the whole family wanted to be together. We lived in a large apartment that my grandmother had with my two uncles, although they were only there sporadically as far as I can remember. I think the place was at number 3 on a street called *Zielona*,[5] which means *green*, and was later changed to *Sarego*.[6] And it was there, on

---

5 According to Polanski's father, it was number 25.

6 The street has been named after Józef Sare (1850–1929), Polish architect, vice president of the city of Kraków, and congressman of the National Assembly, since 1932. Before that and as far

that street Zielona, that my father decided we had to go to Warsaw, that we would be better protected if we took refuge there.

First, he sent my mother, my sister, and me to Warsaw. I remember that rushed departure very well. We took the train. I remember it well because it was a very beautiful summer day. And just before—a day or two before—I was by the Vistula where I'd caught a very beautiful butterfly. One of my uncles showed me how to place it under a glass jar to put it to sleep and then how to pin it on a cork. I didn't want to be separated from this trophy. It was something I carried around with me. I remember that my mother had a few suitcases, as well as a hatbox, and we left Kraków at night. My father and my uncles had decided not to follow us . . . As was happening in France, there was a kind of exodus—toward the east. I don't know which direction people took in France—probably the opposite—but in Poland it was of course toward the east because the Germans were coming from the west.

The Bombings

And so, there I was in Warsaw, which turned out to be the worst place in Poland you could imagine, because that was where the Germans went all out. There were daily bombings, starting with the National Theatre. I don't know why. I learned about it much later—much, much later, actually, when I was

---

back as 1882, it was called Zielona, and that was the address that appeared on the ID card of Polanski's father when he was at the concentration camp Mauthausen.

doing research for my film *The Pianist*. But what I remember as a child is mainly where we took shelter: it was in the cellar.

The apartment my father had rented for us was in a modern building and not completely finished. It was very new and smelled of paint. But then, so had our first apartment in Kraków even though that one was completely finished. It's definite that we were the first tenants for the one in Warsaw. Nor was it very big. I think we had a small entranceway and one or two rooms and a kitchen. Every time an air raid siren sounded, all tenants would go down to the shelter, which was, in reality, a refitted cellar with wooden benches. The hardest thing for me was my mother not letting me take off my shoes, because she was afraid that in case of an attack, we wouldn't be able to leave quickly enough, couldn't flee, or run. And that bothered me a lot, because I slept half on her lap and half on one of those benches.

People were terribly afraid of gas attacks, so most were equipped with masks. Some had none, and that was the case for us. We were told we had to carry gauze, on which we were to pour a foul-smelling liquid that we were to apply to our faces in case of a gas attack. Fortunately, there weren't any while we were there, although our building was hit by a shell that struck a window on a neighboring floor. And strangely enough, for some reason, the tenant of that apartment had refused to leave her home and was killed. She was, I believe, the only person who didn't want to come down to the shelter, and the shell made a big hole right below her window. That was my first experience of the bombings, which would last for two weeks or more.

Hunger and Loneliness

During the period when the Germans entered Warsaw, we suffered a great deal. There was nothing to eat. My mother was often absent because she was trying to find food. Since there were a great deal of bombed-out shops or factories, she sometimes managed to bring back something. One day, for example, she found a big jar of pickles. Giant gherkins. We threw ourselves on them; but after a while, of course, we felt an absolutely horrendous thirst. Nor was there water. You had to go a great distance to fetch it from pumps that were often broken but which leaked water that could be collected. Lines of people holding a great variety of containers would form in front of them.

One day, my mother came back with sugar that she'd collected from a destroyed factory. It was mixed with sand, so she diluted it in a little water. Then she dissolved it and strained it through a cloth sieve. We ended up with sugar, like in the old days: large chunks rather than crystals. And with that, some flour, and another ingredient I don't remember, she made cakes to sell in the street. I was struck by a person like her suddenly showing a new side I hadn't known she had. This rather elegant woman was taking care of the family. And now we'd discovered she had a lot of resourcefulness that could be useful at such moments.

My father wasn't with us in Warsaw. He'd left with that exodus of men heading toward the Russian border.[7] When Poland

---

7 I don't remember exactly when he returned. I've asked my father to write me about all of that, which he has done. See page 62.

capitulated, there was nothing else to do.[8] All these people, all these men, who were heading east to flee and, eventually, resist, were dispersed.

And it was hard; we missed him a lot. Particularly when my mother was away. Those moments were very painful. I remember my sister telling me, "Sleep, it will pass more quickly." And indeed, I'd fall asleep and my mother would wake me up. And those were fantastic moments when she came back. But one time, we opened the door and there was a man, a woman, and one or two children. They settled in our entrance hall because it was where they'd decided to sleep. It was a very small room. My sister and I were all alone when they appeared, but they stayed anyway.

One day while I was playing alone in the vacant lot in front of the building with the tail fins of a bomb or a shell—that thing with fins at the end, which I don't think was dangerous and was one of the few trophies I'd found—I saw a crouching man with open arms, a few hundred feet away. It was my father.

---

8 Nazi Germany invaded Poland on September 1, 1939. On September 17, in accordance with the secret protocol of the Ribbentrop-Molotov Pact, the USSR attacked from the east. On September 22, the Allies organized a joint parade in Brest-Litovsk with the participation of General Heinz Guderian and Lieutenant General Semyon Krivoshein. Warsaw capitulated on September 28, after which the two allies established a common border and signed the German-Soviet Frontier and Friendship Treaty in Moscow, which included secret protocols. In present-day Russia, mentioning these facts is subject to criminal penalties. The final battle occurred on October 6 (Battle of Kock). Poland never formally surrendered.

I ran toward him. Standing, he took me in his arms and kissed me. I immediately began telling him about our life and imitating the air raid siren—two notes, an unbroken one and a modulated one.

It was a new era for us. First, my father managed to evict our squatters. And then daily life began to resume. We were surrounded by enormous ruins. One day, I saw a Polish army vehicle in them. It wasn't a tank but an armed car with a few haggard soldiers. Then, on either that same day or the next, while walking with my father, we saw marching Germans. My father clenched his teeth and said something like, "Those fuckers, those fuckers," in Polish, of course. We soon moved to another neighborhood, probably because it was more working-class or even cheaper—I'm not sure about the reason.

The Anti-Jewish Measures

At some point, my parents decided to return to Kraków. We moved back in with my grandmother. And that's where I started school. I was at the age when children needed to be sent there, but it didn't last long. Soon after, they moved all the Jews into a neighborhood that became the ghetto, and there was no school there. The laws against the Jews came gradually. That's an important point, because quite a few people who learn what happened wonder why the Jews didn't react. They don't understand how such things occur. It wasn't as if one fine morning came around and the Jews were threatened, leaving them time to react.

The worst didn't come immediately. Jews weren't able to organize. It started with banking and money problems. A Jew could no longer have a bank account. Given my age, I don't really remember such things very well, but I heard about them from my parents' conversations. Bits and pieces of what was happening penetrated my child's mind.

At any rate, the first measure I clearly understood was the wearing of the armband with the Star of David. It was a white armband that had to have precise dimensions, and it was very "Teutonic" in style. I don't remember the width very well, but I think it had to be a little more than three inches wide, and the star was blue. It was made of two overlapping triangles in a way that was quite difficult to draw. Since I'd been very small, I'd always drawn, and I'd always heard that I did it very well. Encouraged, I drew as much as possible. But I had a lot of trouble drawing that star. The reason was because it was made with a stencil. As a result, it was difficult to replicate. Even today, when I try, I make a mistake. So that's the first thing I took on, the armbands.

One day, my father came home with blood flowing from his ear. He'd been struck by a German officer because he hadn't saluted him. Jews were obliged to salute Germans when they passed them.

The Transfer to the Ghetto

We were forced to move. This happened after about a year or less—somewhere between six months and a year. I don't remember the exact dates, but they're easy to verify. Contrary to what many people think, the neighborhood where they put the Jews was on the other side of the Vistula in a part of Kraków that was not, in fact, the old Jewish quarter.

All Jews were forced to go into the perimeter that was assigned. The Poles, Cracovians, who weren't Jewish had been forced to move out beforehand to free up that part of the city.

I think we were allowed to take almost all our belongings with us. That was because it wasn't a closed ghetto yet but just the place where Jews were allowed to exist. They couldn't live elsewhere. Previously, many of them had lived in a very old quarter known as Kazimierz and named after King Kazimierz the Great, who'd brought the Jews there in the fourteenth century and where there was a very old synagogue. Like the others, this neighborhood was emptied of Jews who were all forced to cross the bridge and settle on the other side of the Vistula. But at first there was no wall. We lived in cramped apartments because they always housed two, three, or more families. My father dealt with the situation quite well. At the beginning we had two rooms with a small kitchen. There were only two families in that apartment, I believe. We saw little of them, which was good—well, I wouldn't call it "good" today . . .

The building was on the corner between Rękawka Street and a large square with a church. One day, my sister called me to the window and said, "Look." They were building a wall between our building and the one opposite, blocking access from the square to our street. And I understood that they were walling us in. We both wept.

Another era had begun: this was the real ghetto. I would later see that they'd cemented the outside of the wall and coated it with roughcast, turning it gray. It was a finish that you could even say was quite elaborate, with a crenellation at the top of the wall. On our side, they left the wall's exposed bricks. All the walls of the ghetto were like that.

The Deportations and the Perimeter

The ghetto was divided into two parts. A main street crossed the entire ghetto and a tram passed through the middle without stopping. They'd made a kind of wooden footbridge about six feet wide that passed over the tram's power lines. In Kraków, people taking the tram could see the inhabitants of the ghetto, and we could see them.

There was the same situation in Warsaw, but at the entrance where the tram passed, the Germans had installed a large gate made of wire mesh that opened in front of the tram and blocked the passage of pedestrians, then pivoted so that people could cross again.

At a certain point they began to deport people from the ghetto. The population had already decreased. After each roundup, they'd progressively reduce the perimeter. They'd free one part of it and send people to live in the other. When they did that, they no longer rebuilt the wall and would put up barbed wire. As a result, we ended up with a ghetto that was practically surrounded only by barbed wire, despite a few places where sections of the wall remained.

They didn't deport the inhabitants of one part or another of any particular neighborhood, nor entire families, either. They took people at random and separated families. That's how they took my mother, for example. My mother was the first to go.

Daily Life Under Threat

There was no school in the ghetto, but since it was still a city, life continued. There were a few small shops, one or two cafes or restaurants, and a kind of satirical cabaret—at least at the beginning.

I'd received a wonderful gift from one of my uncles. It was a small sled. In the winter I had fun with it since this part of the ghetto was on a hill. In the summer, I hung out with friends on that rocky hill just behind our street.

We had problems getting food. It was difficult. But we never developed full-scale famine as happened in Warsaw, where the ghetto existed for a much longer time. The Kraków ghetto was eliminated before people started dying of hunger. Moreover, the Germans deported people from the provinces into the Warsaw ghetto, even those from abroad who'd already been deprived of everything and were often undernourished. They'd put them in this ghetto without any means of survival. That didn't happen in Kraków. After I fled,[9] I spent most of the War in the Polish countryside. It was there that I learned through village rumors that there had been an uprising in the Warsaw ghetto. I had already been in the countryside for what must have been a year or two.

My grandmother didn't live in the same apartment as us. She was in a very small room on the other side of the ghetto. I don't know how she got that place to live. It was probably about forty or fifty square feet in size—something like that. This was my father's mother. My mother's was Russian. I don't remember her or where she came from, but it was probably somewhere in Russia.

One of my three paternal uncles[10] was in the ghetto, and

9 After the liquidation of the Kraków ghetto, on March 13 and 14, 1943.

10 Bernard (Benek) (1905-1945?), Dawid (Dudek) (1908-1946), and Szymon (Stefan) (1912-?).

another was hiding outside. He arrived at the beginning when you could still come and go freely. I saw him for the last time in the ghetto with his future wife, and then he disappeared. The future wife was Jewish, but she looked very Aryan, not at all Semitic. She hid him in an apartment for the entire length of the Occupation.

During her visits with my uncle, this same aunt taught me how to say Catholic prayers. This was because every time a deportation from the ghetto was about to take place, a rumor would start to circulate, and we would more or less know it was going to happen. Two or three times, my parents placed me outside the ghetto with a family of my father's friends, the Wilks. I even took their name. Later, they found another family in the suburbs, living on a kind of semi-farm where I was supposed to stay. My father paid them for it, and I brought my little suitcase with my personal possessions. However, after a few days, these people said they couldn't keep me—I think because it was too dangerous. I was brought back to the ghetto without the suitcase and without the money my father had advanced. Since I didn't want to be with strangers, I was very happy about it. It had been so unpleasant. I'll never forget the first night. I was lying in a small, raised bed in some kind of shop. This was no farm; it was a country house in the suburbs. The man, who was probably the head of the family, made barrels in a large courtyard. It was the first time I'd ever been separated from my family for several days like that . . .

During that period when we were still in our first apartment, I'd started to wet the bed. And when I was placed with this family, my only worry was the possibility of falling asleep and doing it again. Talking about it was traumatic because my parents would say, "A big boy who wets his bed . . ." I certainly didn't want to piss in bed, but I always dreamed that I was going to the toilet and would wake up and realize I was in my bed.

Checks and Arrests

At the very beginning of the Occupation, even before the ghetto existed, we had to hand over our typewriters. My father was forced to give up his. Once the ghetto existed, things got even worse. At one point, everybody had to hand over every piece of fur in their possession. I think my mother had one or two fox furs. My grandmother had an inexpensive fur coat . . . That was all the fur we had. Two of my uncles, however, were furriers. I don't remember what the third, Bernard, did for a living. But for the two others, it was their trade. I never found out if they had to give up everything. I remember seeing a line of people coming to deposit what they had. Some even brought eiderdowns! You know, when there's a rumor like that, it spreads by what's called the grapevine. And it ends up with absurdities. They didn't ask them to give up feathers, just furs.

We weren't allowed to keep food, either. We could buy it, but only what we had the right to consume. We were warned that there would be a search, that they were going to do an inspection. My mother had baked some small rolls. At the time, we had a small kitchen and a room where we all slept. Originally, we'd had two rooms, I think. After that, it was reduced to one room and a small kitchen. It was there, before the story of the bread rolls took place, that they came looking for my sister. They absolutely wanted my sister, although I don't know why. My mother hid her in the bed. They didn't find her.

The day of the food inspection, two German officers came.

One of them was holding a riding crop. My father had already told my mother to hide her bread rolls, but she had wanted to get rid of them completely. Her idea had been to crumble them up and throw them in the toilet. Finally, she put them in a kind of round hatbox and placed it on a suitcase on top of the wardrobe. At first the Germans followed her into the kitchen. She showed them everything. We stayed in the other room.

They spoke German. My mother and father spoke German. I think my father stayed with us to draw up the inventory of the things we owned that they'd told him to do. And then they joined us in the other room, where we were. They looked everywhere, and strange as it may seem, one of them went directly to that hatbox, which he nudged with his crop. It fell open and revealed all the bread rolls inside. I don't remember exactly what happened. My emotions probably erased the memory of that moment, but I do know that nothing happened. He laughed sarcastically and kicked it, or something like that. The other officer played with my little teddy bear and left with it—I don't know why. And that was the end of my bear. But it stopped there; nothing else happened that day.

There was a much more intense moment when they came to get someone in the building. We turned off our lights and could hear them on the stairs. I was sitting in front of the stove (back then, every room had one of those ceramic coal stoves in the corner). The little door to the stove was open. The red light it threw was the only one on the wall. I was sitting in front of it, my father a bit behind. And I don't know why, but I drew a swastika on the wall with my saliva. And my father said, "Are you out of your mind or what!" He used his own saliva to change the shape of my drawing. At that moment, we heard terrible screaming; they were dragging a woman down the stairs. And then—I don't know how many more. The woman was screaming, and the Germans were bellowing. And then, well, after that, they left. That's how it all ended. I remember it as the first moment that really disturbed me. The next episode of violence occurred when I went to see my grandmother.

Witness to a Murder

My parents always wanted to send me to see my grandmother, and I had no desire to go. That was the case even though I'd really enjoyed her cooking when I was little and we lived at her place, or when my parents went away and left me with her. She had an old scale, and I'd even planted a little bean in a pot on her windowsill. There were also those Jewish holidays in front of the building or in the courtyard, when we made little huts from fir branches. But now, I was older and what interested me more was playing with my friends. Specifically, I had a neighbor friend who was motherless and whose father was very hard on him. He also looked after a little sister. I wanted to stay there with him, but my parents told me, "You have to go visit grandma."

My grandmother always asked questions: "Tell me how daddy is. And mommy? Do they argue?" It was the kind of questions grandmothers love to ask children that annoy those children to death. And so, I went to see my grandmother.

On the way back, the street suddenly started to empty. Not understanding why, I looked around. And then I saw a column of women walking in my direction on the other side of the street. They were being accompanied by Germans—or rather, guarded by the SS. They were walking very fast, and I kept watching what was happening. At the end of the line was an old woman who'd fallen on all fours and was practically crawling on them. She would raise herself up and babble something in Yiddish that I couldn't understand. But what she was doing was pleading with the young officer behind her. And then she went back to walking like that on all fours and, suddenly, the officer pulled out a pistol and shot her in the back. Blood came—not like a spurt but like a drinking fountain. A little ball, a little geyser—yes, like that. Then it disappeared, and she fell. I was petrified. I hid in the house right behind me. There was a wooden staircase. I found a nook under it and stayed there for quite a long time. It was the first time I'd seen something of that nature. And it was precisely around that time that I started wetting the bed. I don't know if it was related to that. A psychoanalyst would say it definitely was, but I'm not so convinced. Children have periods when they wet the bed without a definite psychological reason.

That day, I saw with my own eyes what I'd heard talked about around me, because all the adult conversations were only about scenes of that kind. I knew what was happening, but I'd never seen it. Then I did.

Ghetto Society

At the beginning, it wasn't very difficult to get a permit to leave. Then the situation changed. My mother could leave the ghetto easily because she worked at Wawel Castle, where the governor lived. What was left of Poland was now called the General Government, and the governor was Hans Frank. My mother was one of the cleaning women in the castle. There were probably about a hundred.

They'd fetch Jewish women from the ghettos to work for the governor. It was an enormous palace with hundreds of rooms. There were offices and living quarters for the German occupying forces who were working for this government. It took a lot of people to keep all of that going. The women from the ghetto marched in ranks to go to work there in the morning.

My father worked in a factory. People from the ghettos often worked on the outside. In the morning, they were marched in columns—sometimes carrying their tools—to their workplace. They returned in the afternoon or evening. The children were left to their own devices. At least at the beginning, there was the semblance of a normal life. People were locked up, but they were living. There were richer people and those who weren't so rich; poor people and people with no means at all—even beggars. I most vividly remember an old beggar woman who was a bit crazy and hung around in the streets. We made fun of her a little. Children can be quite cruel. She would shout in Yiddish, "*Shtikl broyt*," which means, "A little piece of bread!" I remember that *shtikl broyt*, as well as the noise she made, which sounded something like, "*Siiiii siiiii*," and made all of us laugh. But there were also people who had means and were considered rich—for example, some klezmer musicians from the Rosner family who worked in a kind of cabaret. One of my friends, Richard Horowitz, who survived all that, is from their family. He's a great photographer and graphic artist who lives in New York.[11]

---

11 A 2021 documentary film by Mateusz Kudla and Anna Kokoszka-Romer, called *Polanski. Horowitz. Hometown* (French title: *Promenade à Cracovie*), follows Roman Polanski and Richard Horowitz through the city of their childhood.

Richard was small at the time. I remember the day of his third birthday. I was invited to his place, and there was hot chocolate. He didn't want to drink it. That was one detail that always stuck in my mind: Richard not wanting to drink chocolate! I often joke to him about that for a laugh, the fact that he didn't want to drink chocolate in the ghetto. He doesn't remember it, and hearing about it annoys him. Apart from that episode and a few other encounters, I didn't see him for the rest of the War. Just after the Liberation, I ended up living with his parents.

Our Residence

These several episodes happened early on, when I was living on Rękawka Street at the edge of the ghetto. I will go back to describing our house. When they built the wall, they of course closed up the entrance to the free side. They also threw out the people who lived on the ground floor. Then they dug a hole into the side of the house facing the ghetto so we could still enter. We had to go in through the cellar, actually. The people from the ground floor who had been thrown out had left behind a lot of their belongings in the basement. Through my child's eyes, it was like a first notion of what remains behind after someone has disappeared. And it would repeat as time went on and they arrested more people, leading to the reduction of the neighborhood's perimeter once again. I return to this because, during the first roundup, when they emptied the part where we lived, among others they took my friend Paweł, the neighbor who was a bit older than me and whom I liked so much. His disappearance was the first of the wounds that were to come. After he disappeared, I dreamed about him a lot.

I believe my grandmother was the next to be taken, or that may have happened a bit later. We were sent to the other side of the ghetto, to an apartment whose inhabitants had been deported. It had been emptied, but when we moved in, we found ourselves there with several families. There were a lot of us living there, but the space was large. I was in one room with my mother and father. There was also another couple in the room with a little boy named Stefan. His father was an architect. Stefan was smaller than me, blond, and really quite cute. And finally, there was an old man with a dog named Fifka, I remember. Beyond our large room, in the other bedroom, there were a lot more people.

Our quarters were extremely cramped, but that hadn't stopped my sister from creating a corner for herself with a little balcony! She'd arranged a small space separated by a large wardrobe, and as a curtain, a bedspread. There wasn't much beyond the space for a bed, and on the back of the wardrobe, she'd glued photos of movie stars because she was crazy about the cinema. She also had magazines whose names I don't remember—*Screen*, perhaps, or *Cinema*, something like that—and she had lots of photos. She was the one who took me to see films in Kraków before the War, when I was very small. I think she was about ten years older than me. Before the War, she was already a teenager. I have her to thank for my first encounters with the screen.

Through our new lodgings, the rumor of a new wave of deportations quickly spread. I left the ghetto. Getting out was very easy for me; sometimes I even went out with friends, without my parents being aware of it. On the rocky Krzemionki hills behind Rękawka Street, there were holes under the barbed wire . . . We were very small . . . It was possible because there was no one to see us at the back of the ghetto. We would crawl under there and find ourselves outside. All of this is very well documented in the Ghetto Museum in Kraków.

The Polish Pharmacy

There were quite a few bizarre, sometimes absurd, occurrences under the German Occupation. For example, the Germans allowed a non-Jewish Polish pharmacist named Tadeusz Pankiewicz to keep his shop in the center of the ghetto. There were, I believe, one or two employees working there, who came in from the city every morning.

He was a very good man, and very quickly the pharmacy became somewhat of a meeting place for the Resistance. This is described by Pankiewicz in a book published after the War called *The Kraków Ghetto Pharmacy*. I don't know if the book has been translated into French, but it was published in Poland.[12] I only read it fairly recently because I didn't know that this book existed.[13] Moreover, after the War, I wasn't at all interested in that subject, until the moment I decided to make *The Pianist*. The only other time I revisited those years was in 1984 to write my autobiography.

---

12 *Apteka w getcie krakowskim by Tadeusz Pankiewicz*, published in 1947.

13 Translator's Note: The book does exist in English: *The Kraków Ghetto* by Tadeusz Pankiewicz, translated by Garry Malloy. It also exists in French translation: *La pharmacie du ghetto de Cracovie* by Tadeusz Pankiewicz, Actes Sud, 1998.

The Roundups and the Arrest of My Mother

While we were in the new apartment that had been assigned to us, a rumor spread that there would be another "action," which is what they called the roundups. I don't remember how I got out—whether it was by using a permit my father was able to obtain. I do know that my parents went to great trouble to get me out of the ghetto and take me to the Wilks whenever it was necessary, whereas I could actually get out on my own whenever I wanted. Because that was during the first period when we were still on Rękawka Street, I never told them. I would go out secretly to a shop not far away to buy stamps with the few pennies I had. Once, when I was with another boy, the shopkeeper asked us without malice, "Are you children from the ghetto?" It scared us so much that we stopped these excursions.

The way I looked passed very easily outside the ghetto. My hair was light-colored, and I truly did have the features of a little Polish boy from the countryside. Because of the rumor, I had to go to the Wilks for a day or two. I spent the night there, and it was my father who came back the next day to get me and bring me back to the apartment. We were walking across the Podgórze bridge, which was very close to the ghetto. When we reached the middle, he stopped. He told me they'd taken Mom and burst into sobs. I didn't, and I told him to stop, because people would notice. So, he forced himself to stop crying and we went home. They had also taken my grandmother. I learned later that she committed suicide. She had some poison and had said she'd never let herself be taken by the Germans. They also took little Stefan's parents.

They did not take my sister. They came looking for her, but she wasn't there. I don't remember where she was hidden.

I found out that my mother had said, "Take me . . ." We stayed in the same apartment we'd been living in, but not in the same part of it; they'd reduced everything yet again. My father left for work at dawn. I stayed in the room with an old man who also worked in the morning. He made his tea, and I stayed in bed. While drinking the tea, his false teeth made noises that were unbearable. And there as well once more were lots of things that had belonged to the people who'd been deported. They were all piled up in the bathroom—a mountain of stuff—and I found a scooter, which I took and played with in the street. One day, a woman stopped me. "But that's so-and-so's scooter . . ." I don't remember the name. And I answered, "No. Now it's mine." I don't remember how that ended, but I think she took the scooter away from me.

Stefan, my father, the old man, and many people I didn't know remained at our residence. There was one more roundup—one of the last. And then I left. I begged my father to make sure little Stefan was taken care of. The Germans liquidated that part of the ghetto, and we went to take refuge in the closet-sized room where my grandmother had lived. From then on, my father, little Stefan, and I lived there.

My sister Annette[14] wasn't with us. I don't remember where she was arrested because they did take her, but that happened later. She'd had a boyfriend when we were all still together in the large apartment with the dog Fifka. She was very much in love with the boy. They were working together in a garden and kissed. When a German saw it from afar, he fired at them. The

---

14 Annette Katz-Przedborska, Roman Polanski's half-sister, was a daughter from her mother Bula Katz's first marriage.

boy got two bullets in his stomach but survived, only to die later. From that moment, Annette became a completely different person. I think the memory of that boy stayed with her for life. I remember him, too.

The Final Return to the Ghetto

After a new roundup, I went back toward the ghetto. From afar I could see that it was surrounded by Germans. At a good distance past the barbed wire I was looking through, I could see where I'd been living with my father and little Stefan. A German was standing guard there. I slipped under the barbed wire without him seeing me and entered the ghetto.

There, right next to our place, was next to nothing; a tiny stationery store. We knew the owners; the store was in the same building as we were. Recently, I tried to find the exact spot. It's not possible because so many things have changed.

That day, the weather was very nice, quite hot. I reached the place where we'd lived. Nobody was there. No one in the courtyard. But there were belongings scattered on the ground. The stationery shop was open, but the owners weren't there. So, I went in. Everything was neatly arranged: the pencils, colored paper, all those treasures for a child. True, it was very small, but there were things I could take, or rather, things I could have taken. "What good is all this to me now?" I thought. I looked to see if there was any money in the cash register. None. I went back out, looking for my father, of course.

Further on I saw a group of people in front of a house being led by a German, so I went over there. I went to join them because I wanted to be with someone, and because all the other homes had been completely emptied of their inhabitants.

After joining them, I asked a man, "Where are you going?" He answered, "Where are you coming from?" I said, "But I wanted to get back to . . ." He insulted me, called me an idiot. Thinking about it now, I realize they were probably people who'd tried to remain there and hide and had been rooted out by the Germans from that part of the ghetto. The German wasn't even paying attention to me. He was short and chubby and was holding some papers in his hand. He looked like a schoolteacher with glasses. There was also an *Ordnungsdienst*,[15] a Jewish policeman who was a member of the Jewish Order Service.[16] They were the ones who were normally supposed to handle affairs inside the ghettos. The Germans wanted to give all of it an appearance of normality.

The Liquidation of the Ghetto and the Escape

They took us to the central square, where the Polish pharmacy still stood. It was called Plac Zgody; it is now Ghetto Heroes Square (Bohaterów Getta). This paved market square was then at the primary entrance to the ghetto and the guards' building—the guards of the ghetto.

On Plac Zgody, there were hundreds—or thousands—of people crammed together. The Germans were doing what they

---

15 *Jüdischer Ordnungsdienst (OD)*. The service of the Jewish Order. When the ghetto was set up, the OD had an office established at 37 Józefińska, in Podgórze, a district of Kraków.

16 *Translator's Note:* During World War II, the Jewish Order was the police force created by the Nazis to ensure German orders within the Jewish ghettos. These police operated under the authority of the Jewish Councils (Judenräte) and were drafted from the ghetto.

called the *Umschlagplatz*, or final selection. Some of the arrested people had been there for I don't know how long—at least twenty-four hours or more. I think I'd returned to the ghetto at that moment because I thought it was over or something like that. But there was a crowd on the square, among whom I began to weave through in an attempt to find my father. Some of them were crying, others had fainted from dehydration. I would try to recreate a bit of that in my film *The Pianist*.

The square was bordered by a street guarded by *Baudienst*[17] with buildings opposite. The pharmacy was on one side, the entrance to the ghetto and the barbed wire on the other. They were Poles in a gray uniform . . . I think they were the *Baudienst*—for us, that's what they were, at any rate. And it was there, while looking for my father, whom I didn't find, that I suddenly came across little Stefan, who was all alone. I grabbed him by the arm and said, "We have to get out of here." There were Germans waving papers and shouting. Suddenly, an officer arrived in the sidecar of a motorcycle. The others saluted

17 *Baudienst* (German for "construction service"): a forced labor organization created by the Nazis on the territory of the General Government, in occupied Poland. Membership in the *Baudienst* was mandatory, particularly for young men. In addition to construction activities serving the German army, *Baudienst* workers were forced to participate in the construction or expansion of concentration and extermination camps, in the dismantling of ghettos after they were liquidated, and in the erasure of traces of crimes. Although in principle unarmed, they were nevertheless required to fulfill the functions of "order" services under German supervision during the liquidation of the ghettos.

him as, clearly, he was their superior. I wonder if they were saluting Amon Goeth.[18]

We hadn't eaten anything since the day before, and Stefan spoke German, so I told him to go ask one of the officers if he'd allow us home to get some bread. We'd come right back. The idea was a completely childish one, and Stefan absolutely did not want to do what I'd suggested. It suddenly occurred to me that I could ask the Polish *Baudienst* who was patrolling the middle of the street. The man stopped, and I asked him whether we couldn't go get some bread. He looked at us and said, "Go ahead." I grabbed Stefan and pulled him along with me. "Don't run! Walk!" We did what he said and crossed the street. Then we went under a carriage entrance. I knew all the courtyards, all the walls, all the holes, all the passages. We ran to the barbed wire and slipped through. We were out of the ghetto.

I would really like to know what happened to that Pole. What kind of life did he lead? Perhaps he's alive. If someone saved my life for certain, it was that boy. He was young, perhaps eighteen years old or a bit more, I don't know, but he truly understood what was waiting for us and let us pass. I then went to the Wilks, who were not thrilled to see that they now had to take in two little Jews instead of just one. We waited a while longer. I think we spent the night at their place.

We went back to the ghetto to look for my father, and it was with him that we stayed until the final liquidation a few weeks later. After that, I returned to the Wilks, but there was no one there. This provided a great pretext for going back to

---

18 See page 140.

the ghetto, but when I returned, before reaching it, I encountered a column of Jews walking by in rows of four, I think, or six—I don't remember, but probably four—guarded by German soldiers. My father was there, and I started walking next to them. Finally, he saw me, too. He was walking next to one of the Germans escorting them. Although I don't know how he did it, I was impressed by the way he exchanged his place in the rank with the guy behind him. Then he did it a second time. I don't know how they communicated. When I mimed from the sidewalk the gesture of locking a door with a key, he said to me, "Shove off!" I stopped and they left, and then I did too, walking in the other direction. That was the last time I saw my father near the ghetto. From that moment on, it was another chapter . . . I learned later that they shot little Stefan with the other children in the schoolyard.

Separated from my father, I was now alone in the streets of Kraków.

A Series of Hideouts

It had been arranged that the Wilks would place me with a family. My father had left them money and jewelry, really everything he had. With that, they were supposed to pay the host family, who were called Putek. They were janitors in a building occupied only by German officers. It was a good hideout, right next to the German barracks. And it was there (at 3 Kremerowska Boczna Street) that I spent part of that period. They had a small apartment where we lived with their son, whose first name was Mietek.

I saw him not long ago. We didn't talk about that time; you don't. We talked about people. He had an aunt who sometimes visited. She was young, her name was Janka, and she was his mother's sister.

I found myself living with a typically Polish working-class family from Kraków. Mietek began to teach me things I didn't know how to do, like hanging onto the back of a tram. We sold newspapers: that gave us a little money for the movies, which became my passion.

I remember when he took me to mass for the first time. I knew the prayers, even though I'd never been in a church. You had to follow the ritual, make the gestures that the others were making. And that was unsettling for me. I thought about it when I was making *The Fearless Vampire Killers*, in the scene where the professor and Alfred try to imitate the others when they dance the minuet. I quickly learned the service of the mass. No one could realize I was Jewish. Avoiding the traps was difficult.

My name was Wilk. I'd become Roman Wilk.

Did the Puteks know I was Jewish? Mietek didn't know, but of course his parents did. I don't know how long I stayed with the Puteks, but a moment came when they decided to send me to the countryside, to Mietek's father's family. I then found myself with extremely poor peasants. The Polish countryside, as I experienced it there, was truly medieval. Few things had changed for centuries. They had a cottage, a small piece of land—a very small piece.

The Making of a Projector

I had a rather unpleasant experience with Mietek's aunt, Janka, the one who'd brought me by train to the countryside. When I was younger, just before the War, I'd been extremely obsessed with a desire to build a projector. The first one I saw was during the little time I spent in school: it was an epidiascope[19] onto which the teacher would put illustrations to be projected onto the wall. I was absolutely fascinated by it—not by what images it projected but by the beam of light and understanding how it worked.

While we were living in the second apartment, the one with little Stefan and his parents, I met a boy who had a little hand-cranked projector as well as a few little bits of film. Strangely, this film wasn't 16 mm but 35 mm. They were very small reels of *Workers Leaving the Lumière Factory* by the Lumière brothers. At the time, I didn't know what it was, only that he had this toy. I think I gave him my stamp collection in return for his projecting the film for me in the bathroom onto a towel.

When I was with the Puteks, more than anything I wanted to project images. I had a lamp and, at the time, I figured you could project an image with the lens from a flashlight. But first I had to cut a square into the kind of tin box I could find at the garbage dumps. In Kraków, they took the garbage away by horse-drawn cart. To find the dump, I hitched a ride on one of the carts. There I found a box, probably a tea box or something similar. To cut the square where I could put the image to be projected, I perforated the metal with a nail. I did this on the porch at the ground floor. The noise I was making annoyed Janka. We argued, and she threw me out into the street, where

19 Translator's Note: An epidiascope is a device that projects images of transparent or opaque objects onto a screen. It was used in education to project photos, documents, and slides.

I found myself with friends, particularly one named Krupa, who was rather a bad boy. Since I was ringing the bell and she wouldn't open the door, he advised me to stick a match in the doorbell. That's when she said she would denounce me to the Germans, but she never did, of course. Otherwise, I wouldn't be here today.

The Discovery of the Countryside

I wasn't yet ten years old when I arrived in the countryside—a bit less than ten, I think, because the ghetto was abolished in March 1943. Let's just say I was nine and a half and found myself in a part of the countryside called Wysoka, which means "high." There weren't many inhabitants. The village only had three or four houses. The houses were scattered on the hills. Our cottage was quite far from the others. The place was very hilly and very beautiful.

It was the first time I had ever been truly in nature. The very first time had been during a vacation in a place that was near very wooded mountains and where my parents had taken me just before the War. It was the only time I'd gone on vacation to the countryside. The place where I'd been sent this time was about thirty-five miles from Kraków, near Wadowice, the town where Pope John Paul II was born.

Mietek's aunt had accompanied me by train to Przytkowice, then to the village where I was going to live, which was more than five miles from the station. I remember that long walk with my little suitcase as well as the discovery of that countryside and those very Catholic peasants. The Buchała family had three children: a daughter who was a bit slow—I don't know exactly what her handicap was and she was very nice, but she was not normal. The older brother was mean. I don't know what was wrong with him, but he was very short and looked like a dwarf. Finally, there was the youngest, whose name was Ludwik, or Lutek, and who was very nice. He was my friend. I think he must have been six or seven. Their father was very old and a real moron, an idiot. He was a shoemaker from Wadowice. Sometimes he made shoes for the children of the house. No one would have come to order a pair of shoes from him even though he did know how to make them. The mother was one hundred percent a housewife, and she was the real boss. She was very kind, too, a very nice person, not to mention hardworking; in fact, she was the one who did everything.

I didn't go to school. I couldn't register; I would have needed a birth certificate and baptism papers. I had barely learned how to read.

These people were very poor. They had a cow. Actually, the cow didn't belong to them; it belonged to the neighbors who lived a bit further down the hill, somewhere between 1,000 and 1,300 feet away. I had no contact with them, but I remember that one day, I saw someone repairing the roof of their house and hitting it with a hammer. I noticed that the sound that was arriving was delayed, not in sync, and I suddenly had the insight that sound takes time to reach our ears, that it's not instantaneous. That neighbor was named Nicieja.

Movie Newsreels

During that period in Kraków, before going to the countryside, I went to the movies, as I've said. Sometimes I went with

Mietek and sometimes alone. I also sold newspapers. When you're constantly in contact with the printed word, you do learn to read. The subtitles of German films, even without my going to school, also helped me learn.

People said then that you shouldn't go to the movies because it wasn't patriotic. There was graffiti on the wall of the movie theater that proclaimed, "Only pigs go to the movies." I wasn't bothered by pigs. I was fascinated by the projection. Even when I was in the ghetto and the Germans projected onto an outdoor screen set up on a large square outside of it. Some of it was newsreels, and from certain corners of the ghetto, through the barbed wire, you could see them. This was done, I believe, once a week, or something close to that, and we kids clung to the barbed wire and watched German propaganda featuring their great pride, the "Tiger" tanks.

The newsreels also presented propaganda films against the Jews. From time to time, you'd read on the screen, "Jews = Lice = Typhus." There was a lot of typhus, especially in the Warsaw ghetto. And it was the lice that spread the disease. So, they said that the Jews were responsible for the typhus epidemics because of the unhygienic conditions of the Warsaw ghetto. Such shots, of course, can still be found in German and Polish newsreels, in new stories filmed by the Germans. In them you can see absolutely terrifying things that make it clear what was happening. Not to mention that the Germans often even filmed the lice with a macro lens.

While doing research for *The Pianist*, I watched hours of these films. But I only saw from time to time the . . . *Kronika Filmowa* (the news), as it was called in Polish. That was intended for Poles.

Daily Life, Fear, and Loneliness

Let's return to the Buchałas. I'm thinking of that first day I arrived: the children, especially little Ludwik, were very welcoming. We went for a walk in a small forest where I saw mushrooms in the ground for the first time. I quickly learned about country life. It was my job to look after the cow that belonged to the neighbors. It was a heifer, and it was kept at the Buchała's. The hope of the entire family was that this cow would give milk. One day, Mrs. Buchała decided that the cow needed a bull. She sent Ludwik, his sister Jaga, his older brother Marcin, and me very far away with that cow. It took us an entire day to get to the bull. But the cow didn't want him. All of us were very disappointed. We came back at night, I remember, and we were afraid.

At any rate, for the entire duration of my stay, that cow never gave any milk. If there was milk, it was because we'd gone to buy it from the neighbors. And one time, in fact, I was going to get milk much farther down and heard someone calling me from afar. I was on a small path and turned around to see a horse pulling a cart. Next to the peasant was a German soldier, which was surprising, because we'd never seen a German soldier in the village. Because I'd heard someone calling me, I turned around but kept walking. I got the milk from the neighbors and forgot about what had happened. About a day or two later, I was picking blackberries on the edge of a path where there were rocks and brambles. In that place, blackberries and everything else that grows in the woods were the only things that saved us. There were also cherries in abundance as well as other fruit trees growing around the house that produced pears and apples. There was a lot of fruit during the summer.

Suddenly, I heard a whistle and the crack of a rifle. I turned around and saw the cart with the same peasant and the German, who had just shot at me. The bullet ricocheted off a stone. That was the noise I'd just heard. I turned away and ran like crazy, dropping the pot with the blackberries. I hid in the woods and only came out after it was much later. And I never understood why they'd done that. I never saw the peasant or the German again. Today I still don't know whether he shot at me because I hadn't reacted to his calls the day before, or whether he really wanted to shoot at me to amuse himself . . . I don't know.

Daily life in the countryside also included an enormous number of critters feasting on us nonstop: fleas, bedbugs, lice. This was before DDT. Battling that microscopic world was a constant struggle. Life had probably been like that before. We made our flour ourselves using a small mill that we turned by hand. It consisted of a round stone with a hole into which we poured the grains, and we turned the stone with a wooden rod that extended all the way to the ceiling. The flour collected in a container beneath the stone. Then we baked the bread in an oven that resembled what we use to cook pizza today. Such was life in Wysoka.

Mother Buchała knew I was Jewish, of course; but neither the old man nor the children did. And especially not the neighbors' children whom I sometimes played with.

We never undressed and no one ever washed in front of another person. At the time, in that society at least, it never happened. There was no need to undress. They were very careful about that. Each of us washed in the stable.

The house was composed of the stable, the kitchen, and

another room. And there was also a very small shed where I sometimes slept. It was actually the place where we kept the grain and the apples—provisions like that. We three children slept in the main room. The mother and the old one slept in the kitchen.

In the morning, it was Mrs. Buchała's religious singing that would wake me up. She sang psalms. Then we all got up. The first morning, I wasn't expecting it.

I experienced moments there where daily life was extremely difficult, but that particular aspect didn't bother me at all. A child gets used to living conditions, and they didn't depress me. A child is sad because he's separated from his parents. And I was suffering for that reason, so I thought twenty-four hours a day about the moment when we'd be reunited. Even while asleep I thought about that.

My sister Annette was in Auschwitz, in a concentration camp. I believe she was in two camps. My mother went to Auschwitz too, but she was with a convoy that took deportees directly to the gas chamber. Annette was younger and was probably selected for work. My sister never returned to Poland but went directly to France after the Liberation. She never went back to visit afterward.

A Meeting Thirty Years Later

I revisited these places about twenty years after the War. I think it must have been in the 1970s, or close to that. I went there and found the cottage; it was abandoned and the roof was destroyed. Right next to it was also a peasant's house, quite new, looking like a little farmhouse. This was before Christmas. I arrived quite late, and inside the light was already on. There was a Christmas tree, and I knocked on the door. The people were welcoming, and I asked, "Where are the inhabitants of this cottage?" The two houses were literally just three or four meters away from each other, not aligned, but diagonal to each other. The corners almost touched. They didn't have an answer to my question. They told me that the youngest, my friend Ludwik, might be in Silesia. But they had no news from him. They didn't know the family. No one knew what had become of them.[20]

I walked farther down to see the Nicieja's house, then the one where I used to go to get milk. All of it no longer existed: all new houses. The place had completely changed, and it was difficult to find my way around. But the landscape was still very beautiful. Sometimes I meet people who tell me, "I know someone who knew you during the War." I don't believe all that. But I would still like to recount an episode that happened more recently. It was about five years ago. I was given an honorary doctorate from the film school in Łódź. There was a ceremony in which a few rectors from Polish universities participated. Wajda was there, in fact, as well as another filmmaker, because we were also being given a diploma from the city of Łódź. They were all in the respective gowns of their universities for this ceremony. A cocktail party prolonged the evening. A gentleman

---

20 Mateusz Kudla and Anna Kokoszka-Romer, Polish filmmakers who made the documentary *A Walk in Cracow (Polanski, Horowitz. Hometown)* succeeded in finding Ludwik Buchała's son, Stanisław. On October 15, 2020, in Gliwice, he received the Medal of the Righteous Among the Nations in honor of Stefania and Jan Buchała, on the initiative of Roman Polanski.

came to have a drink with me and introduced himself as the rector, or dean, of one of the Polish universities—in Opole, I believe.[21] He said to me, "You know, my grandparents—or my parents . . . my grandparents, I think—knew you while you were hidden in the countryside." "Oh really?" I said. And he said, "Yes, yes, they were your neighbors." And I asked him their name. "Well, they were named the same as me: Nicieja." I was shocked. The very thought that the grandson of these simple people was now a university dean in Poland moved me a great deal.

Reading

In this village, I came across a small trunk. Mrs. Buchała's sister was a schoolteacher. She was the only person from that circle who was a bit educated. She'd left behind a chest with books, and no one was interested in it. In that little room where we kept the grain and the potatoes, I would read. Thanks to that, I progressed quickly. It was a small step forward from what I'd learned by reading newspaper headlines and film subtitles. The first book I read was *The Song of Roland* in Polish translation. There was also a monthly magazine called *Rycerz Niepokalanej*, which means *The Knight of the Immaculate*. It was a Catholic magazine, with inspirational stories, and I read all of them because there was nothing else available. However, the thing that interested me the most was *The Song of Roland* because it told stories of knights and battles. It was translated into

21 Stanisław Sławomir Nicieja (1948-), art historian, rector of the University of Opole (1996-2002), and senator (2001–2005).

an archaic language with lots of words I didn't understand. For example, there was the word *murawa*, meaning "lawn," which I didn't know. Although the blood flowing on the *murawa* always impressed me, I couldn't decode its actual meaning.

Rural Anti-Semitism

It was in Wysoka that I heard about the ghetto insurrection and then about the Warsaw Uprising. Because there were actually two uprisings. First, the ghetto uprising occurred in April–May 1943. It ended with its total destruction, almost no survivors were left. A year later, on the 1st of August 1944, the Warsaw Uprising began and lasted two months. It was during the period when the Soviets were already on the other side of the Vistula. They didn't cross the river, waiting for the Poles to lose the fight. This was an uprising of Poles. I eventually heard about it. People obviously talked about such current events.

I heard conversations about what was being said about the Jews of the ghetto. They mocked them a bit. To think that Jews could fight was an idea that was practically absurd for the Polish peasants among whom I lived. The Jew was necessarily a "little Jew," who could possibly sell low-value items at the market or be a lawyer or a musician, but not someone likely to fight. That was the image of Jews in Poland.

It delighted me that Jews projected another image of themselves, although I couldn't show what I felt. It must not be forgotten that Catholics were the heirs of a thousand years of Vatican propaganda. They thought that the Jews had killed their Jesus Christ. On that subject, their portrayal couldn't be changed. If you'd told someone in Wysoka that Jesus was Jewish, he would have killed you. Worse still if you claimed that the Holy Virgin was Jewish. These were unacceptable notions. And yet, these peasants were very good people.

The Front Draws Nearer

We knew that the War was getting closer to us. There was a moment that was phenomenal for me. I was in the woods, picking blueberries. It was during the summer, with all those noises in the forest you can imagine: flies, bees, bumblebees. And suddenly, those noises began to change a bit, and I understood that there were planes passing by. I looked up, and the entire sky was covered with advancing planes. I understood—immediately, of course—that they were American or English planes, and probably American. And then I began hearing "*Pop, pop, pop,*" as explosions and little balls of smoke appeared between the planes, while the formation progressed straight ahead. I lay down on the ground to watch the spectacle. It was a phenomenal moment because we already knew that things weren't going very well for the Germans and that the Allies were approaching, bringing the front nearer. However, it was still on the other side of Germany. I was afraid for these planes. Suddenly, I noticed parachutes. I didn't see the plane that had been hit, but I saw the parachutes that appeared in the sky. They were descending, descending . . . There was one that was falling practically straight on me! I was certain it was going to land somewhere that was very close. But strangely, the lower it got, the farther it was. Until finally, it disappeared behind the trees. Much later, after the War, I learned what had happened: they were American aviators bombing chemical complexes.[22]

From that moment, Germans began driving through villages by car. It was the first time that we'd seen a car in this village. The first one that came, moreover, ended up getting stuck. The peasants helped push it, which seemed funny and at the same time natural because they thought that a motor car was, in a way, inferior to a horse-drawn cart.

The train was far away—five miles. Little Ludwik had never seen a train, nor an electric lamp. What's more, when I told him that by turning a switch, you could turn on the light, he didn't believe me. He agreed that electricity existed and made light. But he wouldn't hear of being able to turn on a lamp from a distance and never wanted to believe it.

Once, I took him to Przytkowice so he could see the train go by. We walked the five miles. We waited for an hour for the train to come, stop, and leave. Although he saw the train, he wasn't impressed, and I was very disappointed that he hadn't thought much of the locomotive.

---

22 The two Polish filmmakers of *A Walk in Kracow (Polanski, Horowitz. Hometown)* managed to identify the plane and the exact circumstances of the incident, as reported in their film. It was a Liberator B-24 "Hell's Angel," shot down on September 13, 1944. Six airmen perished, and five survived. On Christmas 2024, Roman received as a gift from them a piece of the plane's fuselage and some parachute cords, found with a collector.

Liberation

When the Germans started losing the War, they came in large numbers. They began digging trenches all over the country and, particularly, near the village where I was, but never in the village itself. They weren't the ones wielding the shovels, moreover. Sometimes we saw them because they were directing the work, which was carried out by forced laborers who were foreigners—Spaniards and Italians. I don't know what their status was, whether they were prisoners or not. That was when I returned to the Puteks in Kraków. I experienced the Liberation while I was with them.

Toward the end of the War, everything happened quite quickly. We started hearing news about German defeats. Once again, I saw planes passing by, but this time they were over Kraków. They made the same kind of noise, very low and very distant. And one day, we heard the alarm. We had to go down to the cellar, which was also set up as a shelter. We found ourselves with other people who were passing by chance and had asked to take refuge with us. There were a few men, and one or two women. And we stayed locked up there for, I believe, a day and a night, or two days and a night. I don't remember exactly how long, but it lasted quite a while. There were several air raid alerts, but the atmosphere was quite joyful as we waited for the Liberation.

In this house, only the German officers lived, and some had started to leave so that the house was now half emptied of Germans.

There was a goose with us, too. They cut its head off, and Mrs. Putek made soup from it. During the night—I don't know exactly what time it was, but at any rate, down there in the cellar you couldn't tell whether it was day or night—somebody knocked on the metal door of the shelter, at the top of approximately ten steps. We all looked toward that door and were frightened. But finally, Putek went to open it. But before that, the person knocking had shouted something in German. It was a joke meant to scare us: it was just the neighbor, the caretaker of the building next door, coming to tell us that the Germans had left and that the Russians had entered Kraków. We were filled with incredible joy. We came out of the cellar and went up to the floors above. After being on top of one another in the shelter, we could now take over any apartment. The house was completely empty. All the Germans had disappeared, of course.

When they'd started leaving two or three days before, we hadn't yet really understood why. Or at least I didn't know why. Now I understood. The building was empty. They'd left everything behind including their cognac, their wines, and their canned goods. As a result, we were well supplied for a short time, but soon there was nothing left to eat. Finally, we were reduced to eating the bits of bread we'd saved for the rabbits the Puteks kept in a small garden, behind the house, with a kind of vegetable patch. Some of the bread was—I don't know exactly—a year old. Whether rabbits like it that way I don't know, but in any case, they do eat it. We certainly didn't like it. But after the War, we experienced moments of great hunger.

The Last Bombing

Unfortunately, even though we'd been liberated, one night we were bombed again by a German plane. Right next to the building where we lived there was a large barracks, with a German guard perpetually stationed in front. The Soviets occupied it now, and a sentry guarded the entrance.

A few days after Liberation, I woke up during the night to go to the toilet and heard a plane. I turned on the light, and because there was still a curfew, I thought to myself, "They'll see my light," even though the toilet window looked out onto a small interior courtyard and it was impossible to spot the gleam from outside. Even so, I imagined the worst; and at that moment, I was hurled against the door, which was made of frosted glass, and I flew through it. I found myself in the hallway of the apartment we'd taken over on the third floor of that house. Even though I hadn't heard a noise, I understood we'd been bombed. I could hear Mr. and Mrs. Putek, as well as Mietek and the people downstairs, shouting. We were plunged into total darkness, covered with dirt. There was a lot of earth in the apartment. We went down the stairs in the dark, fearing that the staircase might be cut off somewhere. We couldn't see a thing and were afraid of falling. Finally, we got low enough to be able to enter the basement shelter once more.

The next day, we found out that three bombs had fallen. One had hit the house next door, completely gutting it, and killed a few people. Our house had been hit by the same bomb, but it was barely comparable. The other two bombs had formed two craters in the street, and all the earth from that explosion had been propelled through our windows, which were completely shattered. I had a huge wound on my forearm with a piece of flesh hanging from it. It wasn't shrapnel that had wounded me, but the glass when I flew through the pane. The next day, I went to an emergency room that had been thrown together at the hospital. They cut off the piece of flesh and bandaged me with some paper. There were no cloth bandages.

Hunger and Games

After the Germans left, our misery became total. We were hungry . . . Sometimes, there were army field kitchens distributing soup or bread. These could have belonged to the Soviets or the Polish Army, which had been reconstituted in the Soviet Union. Hunger was everywhere, but despite that, we kids played well because there were enormous amounts of munitions, especially in the rooms of the barracks located next to our place. The sentries let us pass. We came out of the barracks carrying bits of German uniforms and other objects. I found a hand-cranked military siren, and they let us leave with that. There were also big straw boots used against the cold by the soldiers, notably the guards. We came out with them, but the sentries didn't know that they were full of weapons—grenades and parts of rifles. Of course, we played with them. Accidents were common. We also had rockets of all colors that were called signal flares. And one day, in fact, while I was playing with a grenade, I completely terrified myself. Perched on a garage, I threw it over a wall onto a vacant lot, but it didn't explode. My friends and I counted the seconds, and finally, after three or four minutes, decided to go see what was happening. And just as we were going to check, it went off. That's when I decided to stop, but I still played with other stuff. Once, I even got caught by the militia. I wasn't carrying anything important—no pistol or grenade—so they let me go.

The End of the War

One day, I'm playing in the street and hear, "Remo!" When I was born in Paris, my parents had thought that the French version of Roman was Raymond. (It's actually Romain.) Consequently, they called me Raymond, and in Poland, Raymond was pronounced "Remo," which I hated. I'd always been Roman, or Romek, its diminutive. And now there I was hearing, "Remo!" It was Stefan, one of my two uncles who'd survived. He quickly took me away from the Puteks, and he and my aunt kept me for some time.

On May 8, the War was over like everywhere else in the world. I remember that day because my aunt's young sister arrived with a Polish soldier. He was carrying his rifle. Shots were coming from everywhere. People, especially the soldiers, were expressing their joy by firing into the air. We were on a fifth-floor balcony, and he handed me his rifle so I as well could shoot. I hadn't turned twelve yet, and it was an unforgettable moment that I still remember vividly. With the recoil, I fell backward. That's what the end of the War was like for me.

Afterward I was taken in again by Dudek, my second uncle, and his wife, the mother of my cousin. They lived with the Horowitzes, who had survived after their internment in the Płaszów camp, near Kraków, thanks to Schindler's List. That means I then found my young friend Richard Horowitz again. I think all of them were living together in a two-room apartment; but even though we may have been living on top of each other, those were very joyful times for everyone—for those of us who were still alive. People were beginning to return from the concentration camps.

I think it was said that Uncle Dudek had been a Kapo in

the Płaszów camp. There were people filing complaints against him. I don't know if he'd really been one, but I believe so. I can't think of any other function he could have had. In any case, there was a trial. I was, of course, kept out of all that. He was convicted; but at the same time, he had a heart attack. I remember going to visit him in the hospital with my aunt, and I seem to remember that he was paralyzed. I wasn't moved by seeing him because he'd been very hard on me. He would beat me cruelly, and since I was a poor orphan kid, almost anything I did could have been excused.

My Father's Return

My parents still hadn't come back, and I, of course, was impatiently waiting for that moment. I thought of nothing else. And finally, while I was staying at my uncle Dudek's, I came home one day to find a man sitting at the table in the kitchen with him. He was drinking vodka. It was my father, who was tanned and wearing a kind of American army jacket. He had me sit on his lap. At that moment, I already knew all the stories about prisoners from the concentration camps, who often came back sick and died after being liberated. Strangely, the only thing I thought about when I was on my father's lap was whether he was going to survive, or whether he had health problems, like many. At that point I didn't yet know that my mother wasn't going to come back. I was still hoping. But after a few months, we knew that she'd died.

Poland and Anti-Semitism

I'm attached to Poland, which is the country where I spent my entire childhood and youthful years. Despite all the problems of anti-Semitism in Poland, they must be balanced with the fact that many people like me were able to survive thanks to the Poles. Such things balance each other out. In a sense, anti-Semitism in Poland is kind of folklore. The Poles aren't aware of being anti-Semitic. Of course, that isn't to say that there weren't those who profited physically or morally from the misery of the Jews during the War. But they were individuals. You can't say the entire nation was involved. There are, in fact, many Poles who helped Jews during the War.[23]

---

23 The first Jews settled in Poland in the 10th century. The first wave of Jewish immigration in Western Europe dates to the First Crusade. In 1098, fleeing the exactions of Crusaders who were on their way to the Holy Land, they found refuge in Poland. In the 13th and 14th centuries, they obtained exceptional privileges (the Statute of Kalisz, the Statute of Wiślica), which contributed to the growth of the kingdom. Despite obscurantist persecutions, for two centuries Poland remained a refuge for Jews fleeing Western Europe. By approximately 1550, 80 percent of European Jews were found in Poland, which then became the cultural and spiritual center of Judaism. The situation deteriorated gradually with the decline of the Republic of the Two Nations (Poland and Lithuania), leading to its disappearance in 1795. The fate of the Jews was particularly cruel under the Russian Occupation, where the assassination of Tsar Alexander II led to pogroms (massacres, exterminations) and the birth of modern anti-Semitism, symbolized by *The Protocols of the Elders of Zion* (1903), fabricated by the Russian "Okhrana," secret police. At the rebirth of the Polish state in 1918, and despite a wave of pogroms in Polish and Ukrainian territories that followed the Bolshevik Revolution and the wars it engendered, the Jewish population of Poland stayed at three million (the 1931 census counted 3,130,581), 12 percent of whom only spoke Polish.

I didn't tell my father about what I'd experienced. He guessed it, but we didn't talk about it. We had no desire to discuss those things. We wanted to move forward.

If I was questioned, I never said that my mother had been killed by the Germans.

During the War, while I was at the Buchałas, I lived in a very Catholic world. I was strongly attracted by the customs and rites and by the religion. I was practically Catholic. After the War, Jews in Poland were afraid to admit they were Jewish. And as they were very assimilated, there were many who hid their origins. They went on like that, and nobody asked the question. After the War, when I was in primary school, I didn't say I was Jewish, and no one was interested in knowing whether I was. What's more, I kept the name Wilk for some time. I survived this nightmare thanks to the Putek family, the Polish peasants, and that young *Baudienst* who let little Stefan and me cross the street. I will be grateful until my last day to those people for actually having saved my life.

The wave of anti-Semitism provoked a vast emigration to the United States, and those who remained would be exterminated by the Nazis (among the six million victims of the Shoah were 2,700,000 Polish Jews).

Letters to My Son

by Ryszard Polanski

Here is my father's letter, written in 1973, which I mentioned in the Foreword. Our exchanges were never lacking in humor. My father had a sharp sense of humor and rarely missed an opportunity to show it at my expense. He was, of course, right to reproach me for not calling him often enough, but I was in the middle of filming.

Kraków, October 21, 1973

My dear boy!

You've provoked me! Consequently, I must speak to you (even if only in writing) as two adult men would talk. Not as a father with his son, but as a man over the age of seventy speaking to a young man of forty in full intellectual and creative bloom. But not physical—I must emphasize!—because gerontologists claim that a man's physical golden age is between twenty-six and twenty-seven years old.

Read my letter several times, not when you're busy but before going to bed. Treat it like bedside reading, and then put it aside. There are times when a man is seized by what is called *spleen*, or *chandra*, in Polish. When that happens to you, take your father's letter, read it, and remind yourself how much worse it could be, and it will pass immediately.

First of all, thank you very much for your invitation, which we will accept with pleasure. We'd like to go to California, Switzerland, and France to see our relatives and friends.

During our conversation, you said two things that made me furious. The first was, "Every time I call you, you have the flu." True! But you call so rarely—once a year or even less—that it almost always coincides with my being ill.

My father died at forty-two. My brother Bernard (Benek), at thirty-eight. My brother Dudek at thirty-eight. Your father, it seems, was misplaced in the celestial register.

As for your second sentence, "Apparently, dad, you like being sick," I've never met anyone in my life who does.

Let me tell you, young man, that you were never a

hard-nut-to-crack like your father, and you never will be. By that, I don't mean to imply that I was an athlete or a weight-lifter, but I was physically and organically resistant to all ordeals, as few people are. I'm going to describe it to you in detail.

As I've already mentioned, you've reached your forties, a fine age for a man. When I was your age, it was 1943, and my son was ten years old. My child was bedding down on the straw pallets of strangers, and his father was rotting in a concentration camp.

My Path to Mauthausen

They loaded 125 men into each cattle car. The tiny window at the top was blocked with barbed wire, and the sliding door was sealed. In the middle of the car was a metal bucket (like our tin garbage cans) where one hundred and twenty-five guys did their business.

We traveled for four nights and three days (because we often stopped at trainyards); and since it was the middle of August, and the cars were overloaded with human flesh and excrement, the stench was unbelievable.

At some station or other, the railway guards (I don't know who took the initiative) started flooding the roofs of the cars with water. Through that tiny window, we could see that the neighboring car was literally steaming (we couldn't see our own), as if it were on fire.

Once a day, the doors opened and, under SS surveillance, we were given a ladle of what they called soup and a small slice of bread. I remember that at a certain station we stayed stopped for a very long time and that we screamed desperately from the car, "WASSER! WASSER!"[24] The door opened, and an SS man appeared. "Where do you expect me to find some?" he asked. "There's a water tower opposite, which is where the railway men draw water. Quick, take your bucket and go get some."

In great haste, four guys took the bucket full of shit, emptied it into a ditch, made a vague attempt to scrape it with their hands—as there was no other way—and brought back water to drink. We threw ourselves on it as if on a magic spring, each plunging his filthy bowl into the redolent bucket, and lapping up the water in great gulps. Ah, what divine nectar! After a moment, the water was gone, and the bucket had resumed its original function.

I had settled in fairly well, you could say. There was a small crack on the other side of the sliding door (which was sealed from the outside). I stuck my head against it to inhale the air coming through the crack. I folded my legs under me, and I stayed crouched like that day and night. I peed through the crack, as well, and didn't do number two until the end.

When we arrived at Mauthausen, there were several corpses in each car, more than a dozen in some. In ours, there were only six. But I remember an SS man who was at the other end of the platform informing another SS man about the number of survivors. "No more than two survivors in that one!" That meant that 120 people had suffocated—or had died in one way or another. But call it what you will—they were free!!!

After being unloaded from the cars, we covered a few more miles uphill on foot, because the camp was situated on a granite

24 "Water! Water!"

hill. And it was this hill that the prisoners were cutting into pieces: it was what's called a quarry.

My Stay in Mauthausen

They undressed me, and I went to the showers. We were a dozen or so per shower. There was no possibility of actually washing; all you could do was get sprayed. They cut my hair to "zero" length with clippers. Down the middle of my head, from the forehead to the back, a strip the width of two fingers was shaved to the bone. With a razor as dull as a piece of iron, and without soap, they shaved the hair on my chest, under my arms, and at my crotch. I was given long blue trousers with white stripes, like the shirt, which had a collar less than two inches high and two ribbons at the front to tie it. Bare feet! No shoes! That was my outfit for the camp.

The next day, I ran into my brother Benek. I hadn't known that he was there too. He pointed to his legs and said, "Look!" His feet were swollen all the way up to the ankles, like a bluish pumpkin. His heart was already shot.

The following day, with a bowl of soup in hand, I looked for a place to sit. I saw a few men sitting on the concrete, their backs against the wall. As I got nearer, I saw Uncle Woller among them. His bowl was on the concrete next to him. I went up to him and said, "Uncle! Why aren't you eating your soup?" I could see that his green eyes (that was their color) had become glassy! His gaze was lost in space, as if a soulless body were sitting there. "Mundziu,[25] it's over!" he said, then repeated the remark again.

---

25 Polanski's father's first name was originally Maurycy ("Mundziu" is the diminutive). He did not adopt the first name Ryszard until 1945.

And I never saw either of those relatives again my entire life, neither Benek nor Woller.

Work

Four hundred—four hundred men, including me—were assigned to the quarries. We formed four groups of one hundred men each. Each hundred was followed by two men with stretchers, the *Leichenträger*, or "corpse bearers." The work was done running. We went down 186 steps to the quarry and came back 186 steps to the surface,[26] with a stone placed on the nape of our neck and shoulder blade. We did four of these rounds in the morning and four in the afternoon, which meant 1,508 steps down and 1,508 steps back up, all while carrying the stone. To avoid attracting attention, I immediately took a large stone on my neck.

The corpse bearers weren't allowed to come back up without a body. Four corpses came back each time, which made thirty-two corpses per day over the eight rounds. Starting the next day, the deficit was made up with new people.

What bothered me the most was eczema. In the places where I'd been shaved—that is, the chest, the armpits, and "down there," the hair started to grow back, stung me mercilessly, formed pustules, and itched terribly. But since the hair grew back (slowly), the bumps disappeared.

The camp was directly subordinate to Himmler. As he was a cunning fox, to fill the ranks of the SS and the camp guards, he released prisoners, murderers sentenced to long prison terms, or life sentences. Each received a six-and-a-half

26 See the photograph on p. 74.

foot-long leather whip, which they tore to shreds on our backs.

Freed from the Quarry

One day, a transport was preparing to leave for another camp (a sub-camp), which was also part of Mauthausen and was called Linz III. Disregarding the fact that I belonged to another group (the quarry group), I slipped into the barracks where they were issuing clothes. I received striped trousers and a striped shirt, a matching round cap, a dirty white homespun shirt, kind of tattered undershorts, and a pair of wooden clogs for my bare feet. As soon as the wagon started moving, I was overwhelmed by a feeling of great well-being based on having freed myself from the quarry. We stopped about five and a half miles from Linz, in a small camp of fifteen thousand people.[27] The town was called Kleinmünchen. I entered barracks number 5, which housed 200—or sometimes 250—prisoners. The bunk beds were two levels high and 32 inches wide, and each held two people. I got the top spot, which I was supposed to share with another, but those others kept dying. Each time I was supplied with a new one. Bedding consisted of a flat mattress filled with straw (ten blades of grass . . .), a small headboard for two, which was also made of straw, and a dirty gray blanket, also intended for two.

27 The camp Linz III, which opened on May 22, 1944, and was liberated on May 5, 1945, had around six thousand prisoners (according to current sources).

More Work

I was assigned to the H.G.W. (the Reichswerke Hermann Göring[28]). I wasn't sent to the factory floor, but to do outdoor tasks. My first chore was mixing concrete. As there was no mixer—no drum to mix the concrete—we did it by hand. Our group was composed of three people. After pouring four bags of cement onto the ground, we added a certain amount of sand and small river pebbles. We were directed by a German civilian foreman, who poured water over it using a watering can, like the kind for watering flowers or, in Poland before the War, for cleaning sidewalks. We had to shovel up this mixture very quickly to prevent it from hardening; and the more we stirred, the more difficult the work became, since the cement was becoming denser.

Later, also in groups of three, we were ordered to unload powdered coal, which was, in fact, just coal dust. The wagon contained fifteen tons, and the SS guard gave us one hour to empty it. We did it with shovels very far from the wagon, to prevent even the slightest dust from accidentally falling on the rails.

I was sweating and covered in a black, sticky mass almost half an inch thick. I couldn't tell you how much I had in my lungs.

Then I unloaded bags of cement. I took a fifty-kilo bag, put it on my shoulders and around my neck, and carried it a distance of six hundred fifty to a thousand feet; and there, under a

---

28 Translator's Note: *Reichswerke Hermann Göring* was an industrial conglomerate in Nazi Germany from 1937 to 1945, established to extract iron ore from various sites.

kind of vault, we stacked them. Once, an SS guard who was a son-of-a-bitch, didn't like something and stopped me, ordering another porter to put a second one on my back and saying, "Since you do it so well."

Goddamn it! No way! I bent over and walked very slowly so as not to fall. With my left hand I held the sacks, and with my right hand, which was in my trouser pocket, I pushed in my guts so they'd stay inside! I forgot to say that while lifting a large stone in the quarry, I'd ruptured my right groin and gotten a hernia that I still have today. Carrying such a weight, I could literally feel my intestine popping out of my abdomen.

I carried this weight several times. Finally, I mustered my courage, went to see the SS guard, and said to him, "Listen sir, I'm going very slowly with two sacks. With one, I can go much faster than the others, and I'll carry even more than them." He fell for it! All I had to do was run like a man possessed, for fear that this son-of-a-bitch would pick on me again.

Life in the Camp

For the entire length of my stay in the camp, I wasn't given any other clothes. The ones I was wearing were dirty, greasy tatters full of lice. The clogs made holes in my feet, so I wrapped my feet in paper torn from the cement bags. Work at the camp lasted twelve hours a day. One week you worked during the day, the next at night. Fortunately, I was now inside on the factory floor, where the work was already lighter.

When two hundred dirty, stinking bodies teeming with lice sleep in a wooden barracks, you can imagine what kind of air they breathe.

Throughout spring, summer, autumn, and winter, at five in the morning, the gong would sound and we'd all get up from our bunks. The windows were wide open. There was a draft, a tornado! A veritable cyclone. We formed a line and came out of the barracks completely naked to go to the latrines, then to the *Waschraum*, or "washroom." It was a barracks where two guys held rubber hoses and sprayed us with cold water—like a concierge watering a sidewalk or a gardener his lawn. Soaked, we then ran the three hundred meters back to the barracks, where we dried ourselves with a piece of dirty cloth called a towel. Since autumns were rainy, after this run, my legs, back, and neck were covered in mud. I wiped myself with the towel and that was fabulous.

It wasn't being used to make us clean—no German cared about that—but to finish with us as quickly and in groups as large as possible. The same "watering" took place in the evening after returning from the factory. The factory was located one and a quarter mile from the camp, and we made the round trip on foot every day.

After our morning "toilette," we quickly put on our rags, had our breakfast (always standing) and ran to the *Appellplatz*.[29] They would make us stand around and wait there for hours, regardless of whether it was hot, raining, or freezing. Since the Germans were and still are very meticulous, it took two, three, or four hours to calculate the number of *Häftlinge* (inmates). Each SS guard managed several units. Every unit leader reported his prisoner count to him, which he noted, afterward passing

29 Translator's Note: The *Appellplatz* was the roll-call area of a concentration camp.

the total on to the *Rapportführer*.[30] He noted the total number present at the roll call, the number of those going to work, the number of those in the block-hospital (*Revier*[31]), and the number of corpses in the morgue. The latter had to be transported to the Mauthausen crematorium, and all this gave him the total number for the camps. He would have trouble, and the count would be wrong, so we repeatedly remained standing while he counted and recounted, until he finally got it right. Once the count was finished, he reported it to the camp commander (a sixty-five-year-old Austrian who was a former director of a bank in Vienna named Szeperle,[32] a son-of-a-bitch who has departed this world); and only then did we march out to work in close formation, hammering the ground with our clogs.

In March 1945, three Russians escaped from our "crew," but their attempt was doomed from the start. For one thing, they didn't speak German. Secondly, they were wearing striped pajamas. Thirdly, they had shaved "stripes" on their heads. The order was given to hold us all in a field next to the factory until they were caught. We stayed there for forty-eight

---

30 Translator's Note: An *SS-Rapportführer* was usually a mid-level non-commissioned officer who served as commander of a group assigned to manage a barracks in a concentration camp.

31 Translator's Note: "*Revier*" was the term used in concentration camps to refer to the medical facilities for inmates.

32 *Obersturmführer* Karl Schöpperle (1891–1948), originally from the Black Forest, was the architect and director of a professional school. He was the commandant of several of Mathausen's satellite camps. Linz III would be his last. Condemned to death on June 23, 1947, by the American Dachau trials, he was put to death by hanging in 1948.

hours. Without sleep, food, or a drop of water. Anyone who collapsed from exhaustion was shot on the spot, and the bodies were piled up to the side. Since it was cold, we were spared having to stand in regular ranks, so we formed "piles" of fifteen or twenty people pressed back-to-back against each other. There was always one who stayed in the middle for a while, who then came out to let another take his place. In the end, the Russians were captured and hanged, and we returned to our barracks. The hanging ceremony took place with great pomp, and in case you were wondering, everybody had to be present and watch.

My Diet

As I said earlier, in the morning, a ladle of nearly black coffee and a slice of bread; at noon, a bowl of soup (pathetic!); and in the evening, another ladle of coffee. Once every two weeks, a half pat of margarine. No self-respecting pig has eaten as many peelings as I have. In November and December 1944, as well as January, February, March, April, and up to May 5, 1945, my main food consisted of potato peelings.

I bought them for half a cigarette, from those who peeled potatoes in the kitchen. More than once, and to my great regret, they were too thin. I would receive cigarettes as a bonus for my good work. On Saturday, the *Oberkapo* would note "good for bonus," and they were distributed on Sunday. I was sometimes given three cigarettes, sometimes five, and very often, nothing at all.

In the first months of 1945, I had abscesses! If you're wondering what that is, well, on both legs—my calves—holes the size of a wristwatch appeared, from which thick, yellowish-green pus flowed. A bit like that lubricant used to grease car axles. No, I absolutely did not go to the *Revier* (the barracks hospital), God forbid. I tore paper from the cement sacks since they were made of several layers. After throwing away the first that was covered with the most cement, I wrapped my wounds with the others and wound aluminum wire around my leg. Since I had an infinite number of lice, they settled in these wounds. It was warm there, and there were tasty things to eat.

Several times a day, I unwrapped the paper and chucked the lice out of the wounds with a clean little stick, and so on, repeatedly. And in the evening, before going to bed, rather than treating myself to a short reading session, I organized a lice hunt of those that were teeming in my shirt, clothes, body, hair, ears, and everywhere you can imagine. Each time I caught a hundred, a hundred and twenty, a hundred and fifty lice of different colors and sizes. As my body weakened from the lack of vitamins and resisted the cold less and less efficiently, I made myself a vest from a cement bag, just like a medieval knight wearing chain mail. I cut the sack at the sides, shortened it, and made an oval for my head. Today I wear a vest, but back then, I put a cement bag over my shirt. It protected my chest and back, and the sides were comfortable. Nothing hindered my freedom of movement.

Suddenly, an idea comes to mind. I've run around naked so many times on various Appellplätze that I might as well join a naturist club.

But during all that time I never caught a single cold.

"The Stairway of Death" at the Nazi concentration camp Mauthausen in Austria. © Interfolio/LA COLLECTION

It was only very recently that I discovered the photo of the "Stairway to Death" at Mauthausen described by my father in his letter.

In 2002, I was in Israel with my crew to present *The Pianist*. We'd been invited by the Yad Vashem Institute. That was when its director told me that, despite the time that had passed, oral histories and documents from that era continued to reach them. Among these, for example, was the complete file of the inmates of Mauthausen, recovered by the British army, which had participated in the liberation of the camp. The director took us to the archives, where there was an immense file carefully arranged by nationality and in alphabetical order. Two hundred thousand prisoners passed through Mauthausen, ninety thousand of whom were murdered. We immediately found my father's card. I was staggered by the elegance and administrative precision evidenced by these documents. I noticed that my father had falsified his date of birth—he'd made himself six years younger—as well as his profession—he'd claimed to be a locksmith.

KL.:

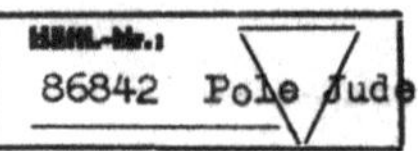
Häftl.-Nr.: 86842 Pole Jude

Häftlings-Personal-Karte

Fam.-Name: L i e b l i n g
Vorname: Maurycy
Geb. am: 28.9.09 in: Krakau
Stand: verh Kinder:
Wohnort: Krakau Zielonastr 25
Strasse:
Religion: mos Staatsang.: Polen
Wohnort d. Angehörigen: Frau Bula geb Katz w.o.
Eingewiesen am: 10.8.44.
durch: Plaszow
in KL.: KLM
Grund: Pole Jude
Verstrafen:

Überstellt

am: ... an KL.
am: ... an KL.
am: ... an KL.
am: ... an KL.
am: ... an KL.
am: ... an KL.

Entlassung:

am: ... durch KL.:
mit Verfügung v.:

Personen-Beschreibung:

Grösse: 166 cm
Gestalt: schl
Gesicht: längl.
Augen: braun
Nase: eingeb.
Mund: voll
Ohren: norm
Zähne: lück.
Haare: schwarz
Sprache: poln. dtsch franz.
Bes. Kennzeichen:
Charakt.-Eigenschaften:
Sicherheit b. Einsatz:
Körperliche Verfassung:

Strafen im Lager:

Grund:	Art:	Bemerkung:

Kl./8/a. 44-500923

Erlernter Beruf: Schlosser
zuletzt ausg. Beruf:
Arbeitsbuch Nr.:
Berufsgruppe:

Ausgebildet in der Zeit ... (Ausbildungslehrgang)
als ... im KL.

Eingesetzt

	vom	bis	als	bei
1.				
2.	"	"	"	"
3.	"	"	"	"
4.	"	"	"	"
5.	"	"	"	"
6.	"	"	"	"
7.	"	"	"	"
8.	"	"	"	"
9.	"	"	"	"
10.	"	"	"	"
11.	"	"	"	"
12.	"	"	"	"
13.	"	"	"	"
14.	"	"	"	"
15.	"	"	"	"
16.	"	"	"	"
17.	"	"	"	"
18.	"	"	"	"
19.	"	"	"	"
20.	"	"	"	"

As you can imagine, my father's letter that you've just read made a very strong impression on me. I mainly felt that it would be a shame to stop there. So, I asked my father to write a sequel. He declined, and I insisted. When I proposed to pay him, he smiled and said, "It's starting to interest me." He went back to work.

In accordance with your request, I'll set down on paper a new series of recollections dictated by my memory, to complete the work begun in California in January of this year.

When we returned to Poland in 1937, we first lived with my mother and my brothers at number 25 Sarego Street.

After a while, we rented an apartment on Urzędnicza Street.[33] In 1939, the situation had become precarious, and it already smelled of war, so we left that apartment to move back in with my mother, who'd always said, "It's war, and we'd do better to be together."

During the first quarter of 1939, Annette moved to Warsaw. She went to live with her aunt—your mother's sister.

At first, she worked in an office as an administrative assistant, and then she became an extra in several films by Misza Waszyński.[34]

---

33 Roman Polanski doesn't remember Urzędnicza Street but does remember, down to the slightest details, an apartment on Komorowskiego Street, in another part of Kraków.

34 Misza Waszyński (Mosze Waks, 1904–1965), film actor and director. In the 1930s he made around forty feature films in Poland, the most famous of which is The *Dybbuk* (1937), the first full-length film in Yiddish. During the Second World War he accompanied General Anders's army and filmed the Battle of Monte Cassino. After the war he worked in Italy and Spain as co-producer of

As is often the case in life, coexistence between the daughter-in-law and the mother-in-law—I'm talking about my wife and my mother—hadn't gone well. As a result, your mother and I decided to move to Warsaw.

A few months earlier, I'd gone to Warsaw, where I'd rented an apartment in a newly constructed house whose plumbing was still unfinished. The owner of the building was supposed to write to me in Kraków about the completion of the work and the possibility of moving in.

She never did. When war broke out on September 1, 1939, the Polish nation scattered like a flock of pigeons being attacked by a falcon.

I never got my deposit back, and when I came on foot from Lublin to Warsaw, I found Mom, you, and Annette in an unfinished house, without any furniture or appliances.

Our newly bought, beautiful furnishings for three rooms and a kitchen, which had been deposited in Kraków in the warehouses of the Hartwig Company, had been seized by the Germans (meaning, the SS).

In any case, we would have lost everything, since Polish Jews lost not only their possessions, but also their lives.

After your departure for Warsaw with Mom, I stayed with my brothers in Kraków.

When I accompanied you to the Kraków railway station,

---

several well-known films (*The Barefoot Contessa*, 1954; *The Quiet American*, 1958; El Cid, 1961; *The Fall of the Roman Empire*, 1964). He was famous for his fantastic stories about himself. Since he claimed aristocratic origins, he was given the nickname "the Prince."

after dealing with the difficulty of getting you settled in a crowded train, Mom said to me, "Will I see you again in this lifetime?"

It was thought that, in case of war, Warsaw, which was the capital, would be the best defended and the least threatened compared to other Polish cities.

However, on September 1, 1939, starting at five in the morning, all the major cities of Poland were bombed simultaneously, and with such efficiency that the War was lost in the first hours of those air raids.

Airfields, stations, railways, telecommunications—everything ceased to exist. The continuation of fighting, resistance, and local skirmishes were only a matter of finishing up for the Germans —just a cosmetic procedure.

Sending you to Warsaw was therefore ill-advised, useless. Yet another thoughtless decision.

The rapid penetration of the German army into the depths of Poland created panic and a hysterical desire for flight among millions of people.

The direction was eastward. On September 3, 1939, my brothers Benek and Stefan and I left the house, abandoning Mom, and set off on foot across Poland.

The day before, Dudek, my third brother, had left with his wife Tosia and daughter Roma on their horse-drawn cart, because Tosia's father-in-law had a bakery with horses and carts to distribute bread.

They returned to Kraków on foot, without a horse or cart. The horse had died, no one was able to pull the cart, and they'd had no choice but to leave it on the road. It was only a wooden cart.

The entire road from Zaleszczyki[35] to the Romanian border was clogged with the most elegant cars, loaded with suitcases and luxury clothes.

And the key to every car was still stuck in the ignition.

Our government was fleeing to Romania, but few were those who had thought to take enough gasoline.

Others saved their lives by leaving everything behind and running on foot, just to cross the border and avoid falling into the hands of the Germans.

Our own luggage consisted of a pair of trousers, a shirt, a towel, two pairs of spare shoes, and shaving equipment.

That's what a fugitive's possessions looked like. Benek, who was more cautious and had taken more things, gradually got rid of them along the way.

During the last leg of the trek, only the single pair of shoes on our feet were left, because we'd thrown away the spares.

We walked day and night until we collapsed from extreme exhaustion.

Direction: Proszowice, Kazimierz Wielki, Staszów, Tarnobrzeg, Nisko, Zawichost, Janów Lubelski, Kraśnik, Lublin.

Starving! Dirty! Unshaven! Sweaty! Stinking!

A heat like that of September 1939 hadn't been recorded for decades.

We slept in the woods, or in ditches by the side of the road, under the constant fire of the machine guns of German dive bombers.

---

35 Zalichtchyky, a town located in southeastern Poland in 1939 but considered part of Ukraine today, has become proverbial because it was used by the Polish elite fleeing to Romania.

Thousands of people died on the road from exhaustion, dysentery, and bullet wounds.

A collective psychosis of flight had set in. You had to get as far away as possible from the German troops—before being shot or taken to camps, etc.

Alas, it turned out later that those who had stayed at home fared better.

After walking for several days and several sleepless nights, I began to become delirious. I staggered as I walked, constantly seeing an imaginary chasm in front of me. I was falling into it, into the depths, until I actually did fall into a ditch at the edge of the forest.

I couldn't say how long I slept, with my two brothers at my side and two other young boys from Katowice that we'd taken on along the way.

Tens of thousands of people passed along the road, like waves of a flooding river. For us, the world didn't exist.

We were completely consumed by lack of sleep and exhaustion.

Walking like this for over 250 miles, we finally reached Lublin.

The five of us occupied an abandoned Jewish apartment on Lubartowska Street.

The most extraordinary thing about all of this is that the owners had left Lublin to flee the Germans, while we had fled Kraków to take possession of their apartment.

As I write these words, I still think about the outrageous errors people made, including myself.

We took the apartment in the evening but didn't sleep a wink all night.

We hadn't slept for fifteen days, and yet none of us went to bed. We remained there sitting, expecting artillery fire at any moment.

It was the night the Germans were taking possession of Lublin, constantly bombarding it with guns of various calibers.

For us, flight was already futile. There wasn't a single town left that wasn't already occupied by the Germans.

Before reaching Lublin, we passed through Zamość, initially bypassing Lublin.

Once we reached the suburbs of Zamość, we discovered that the city was already occupied by German troops.

We had no choice but to turn around and head back toward Lublin, which was still free.

In the morning, after an all-night bombardment of Lublin, the German troops entered the city.

Here is a fact that will illustrate the extent of human stupidity and stubbornness:

In the morning, around five o'clock, we heard all the tenants in the building running down the stairs.

We ran out as well. A group of people, tenants of the building, had collected in front of the entrance.

From a distance, in the morning mist, we could see the German army in attack formation, rifles in hand, barrels pointed forward, ready to fire; that's how you take a city.

Suddenly, in our group, a serious man of around fifty-five or sixty (I was thirty-six at the time) shouted, "Oh, sweet Jesus, it's the French coming to our aid!"

That was when I heard a German officer order, "Alle Männer ins Konzentrationslager!", which means, "All men to the concentration camp!"

I immediately shouted, "Guys, let's split!" and we dashed into the building's cellar.

Bad luck ordained that the building had a huge, monstrous courtyard (which we didn't know about).

It was half the size of Kraków's main market square,[36] and to top it off, there was a wide carriage entrance.

After a moment, we heard the rumble of carts, horses, and soldiers, who had set up their quarters in that same courtyard.

A guard with a rifle was immediately posted at the entrance to control the movements of the inhabitants.

We stayed in the cellar for several hours, until I finally said, "Guys, there's no point staying here like rats, we're going to starve to death."

I climbed the cellar steps to the exit. Through the keyhole I could see soldiers washing in the courtyard while others were cleaning their horses or their boots.

It was relatively calm, and apparently the first roundup was over.

Since I hadn't shaved once during the entire trek, I had quite a beard.

In the darkness, I took my shaving tools out of my bag, took a piss into the bowl, and soaped my beard-covered face.

Shaving was done by guesswork without a mirror, using the sense of touch, and somehow, I managed to get rid of the beard.

I wiped my face with my own shirt, without rinsing, and left the cellar.

---

36 *Rynek Główny* (principal market): an immense, famous location in the center of Kraków.

Someone standing guard accosted me. "Who are you?" he said in German. "I live here," I replied, and I went out into the street.

After a moment, I came back in.

And since it was a large quadrilateral building with a huge courtyard (as I've said), many people were going in and out.

I immediately went down to the cellar and brought my companions in misery upstairs to the apartment.

We made ourselves a good breakfast, because, as our search revealed, the owners had accumulated ample provisions in anticipation of the War.

I don't think they ever imagined they would have to abandon all this and set off wandering on an absurd journey.

Apropos of this, I should mention that the same situation would occur a few months later in France.

Millions, literally millions, of people abandoned their belongings and their houses, fleeing in panic before the advance of the German troops.

The roads were so clogged with civilians that any troop movement was unthinkable.

After breakfast, one by one, at regular intervals, we left the hospitable walls of an apartment whose owner we didn't know.

We needed to look for another hideaway, this time one without a large courtyard.

Later in the day, we moved into a three-room apartment on Chopin Street.

I no longer remember how we spotted that apartment.

We stayed in Lublin until the Germans seized Warsaw and liquidated the remnants of the Polish army that had stayed behind.

When the return of tens of thousands of people to their homes became relatively possible, I said goodbye to my brothers.

They left in the direction of Kraków, I for Warsaw.

I only covered 115 miles . . . I don't remember how long I walked, and it was already October 1939.

I fed myself on carrots stolen from peasants, cooked potatoes, and, if a peasant woman was willing to give me some, a piece of pie and a little whey.

I had no more money, and what I had was worthless, because you couldn't buy anything with it.

So, I dragged myself to Warsaw.

When I arrived at our place, I found you outside, playing in a vacant lot.

When you saw me, you shouted, "Papa!"

I took you in my arms and lifted you up, overjoyed, kissing you. You were six years and two months old then.

The living conditions I found you in were terrible, because the house was unfinished and, to top it off, not a single windowpane had survived the bombings.

You immediately started giving a concert: ATTENTION! ATTENTION! ATTENTION! CHOCOLATE! CHOCOLATE! CHOCOLATE! STRAWBERRY! NARCISSUS! ATTENTION!

These warnings were broadcast several times a day by Polish radio through loudspeakers in the streets.

They were broadcast in a desperate voice by the mayor of Warsaw, Stefan Starzyński,[37] at the very moment the German bombers were approaching Warsaw. The words "chocolate," "strawberry," and "narcissus" were undoubtedly codes indicating the planes' route.

---

37 It wasn't Starzyński who was reading these messages but an announcer.

You kept imitating the buzzing of airplane engines and shouting, "Attention—attention—here comes the chocolate!" It was the chocolate that amused you the most.

Starzyński was arrested immediately after the Germans arrived.

He was imprisoned for months and tortured in an inhumane manner in the prison known as Pawiak, then sent to the Buchenwald concentration camp.

Shortly before the end of the War, he was shot in that camp.[38]

Soon after, we had to leave the apartment and move to a Jewish quarter created by the Germans—the "ghetto."

The ghetto was, for the moment, just an assembly of "subhumans," meaning Jews, in an open neighborhood, meaning it was possible to leave it and go anywhere in Warsaw.

Every Jew had to wear on their left arm a white armband four inches wide with a blue Star of David.[39]

Soon, news spread that the ghetto was going to be closed, that Jews would no longer be able to leave its confines, and that Warsaw would be divided into quarters for Poles and quarters reserved for "superhumans," meaning Aryans of "pure Nordic blood," known as the *Reichsdeutsche*.

One day before the ghetto was closed, my brother Stefan arrived in Warsaw.

In a few minutes, we'd packed our modest suitcases (containing only small things), and, after removing our armbands, left by night train for Kraków.

---

38 Actually, he was murdered at Pawiak Prison in December 1939.

39 That rule was introduced on November 28, 1939.

This rushed departure went off without a hitch.

We settled, for the third time, with our mother and our brothers at number 25 Sarego Street.

Our joy was short-lived, because a few weeks later, the Jews had to leave their apartments and move to the ghetto that had been created in the Podgórze district.

My mother and my brothers were given a small room with a kitchen on Nadwiślańska Street, while we obtained a three-room apartment, intended for three families who didn't know one another.

It was at no. 2 Rękawka Street, and in total there were eleven of us.

Three mothers would cross paths in the kitchen, but taking into account the oppressive conditions created for us by the Germans, the ladies arranged things themselves in a way that avoided any confrontation.

This idyll didn't last. Deportations to the "extermination camps" began very quickly.

In the ghetto, a police force was created, organized by the Jewish municipal councilors and approved by the Gestapo chief, bearing the name *Ordnungsdienst* (order service) or, in short, the *OD*.

By order of the Gestapo chief, from time to time this police force had to draw up a list of people to be deported, meaning a mandatory quota of three, four, or five thousand people.

It was done haphazardly, without any sense or logic, because the Germans knew very well that the Jews would continue to deport one another until their turn came, and then they themselves would be deported.

By surrounding the ghetto with a wall built for that purpose, and by reducing the living space, the Germans made it easy to dispose of the remaining Jewish population until the ghetto was completely liquidated.

Seeing how desperate the situation was becoming, I began to look for a place for you outside the ghetto.

One of my friends, Henryk (Henio) Wilk, and his wife, whom you know well, helped me.

I also urged Mom to leave the ghetto and find shelter outside of Kraków with what were called "Aryan papers."

Nothing about her, not a shadow of a feature, could suggest non-Aryan origins.

She was a very pretty woman, well-built and slim, and she belonged to the Orthodox Christian faith.

She had been born in Russia, in Yelizavetgrad,[40] in the governorate of Kherson.

She spoke Polish and Russian very well. Unfortunately, she didn't want to hear any talk about leaving the ghetto.

She stubbornly repeated: "I'm not leaving you. Wherever you go, I'll go."

All my arguments urging her to save herself and our child were in vain.

From that time on, certain groups of Jews were assigned to the construction of barracks for the future Płaszów camp, where they were immediately sent to live.

To deceive us and make us believe we weren't destined to be exterminated, we were assigned work details.

---

40 Today called Kropyvnytski. According to statistics, in 1897, Jews made up 37.8 percent of the population. Grigori Zinoviev, one of the leaders of the Bolshevik Revolution, and Heinrich Neuhaus, the great pianist and professor, were born there.

The Germans created an *Arbeitsamt*, or "employment office," in the ghetto and issued us cards (certificates) indicating that X. Y. is employed and as such remains indispensable to the economy.

All this was nothing but a perfidious lie, from beginning to end.

Mom's job was cleaning Wawel Castle, and every day she left the ghetto walls with a group of women.

I'm sure you remember that the uncrowned king of the General Government, Governor [Hans] Frank, lived at Wawel.

Every morning, I was given a pickaxe, a shovel, or a broom to sweep the street.

We left the ghetto walls in groups and, depending on the season, took care of the cleanliness of Kraków.

We swept the streets, dug ditches, or shoveled snow to load onto trucks.

Annette, who already had a boyfriend who did carpentry, I think, was responsible for transporting planks.

After a few "actions"—namely, the deportation of a few thousand people to the extermination camps and the execution of a few hundred on the spot—I again asked Mom to go with you.

I explained to her: "You have jewelry—gold, and silver too. You'll manage."

"You'll certainly find work, even if only to keep up appearances. Money runs out so quickly—and you know I'm going to end up in a camp. The ghetto is about to be liquidated."

For the sum of five thousand zlotys, I managed to get hired at the Waks metalworks factory. It belonged to a Jew but now found itself under German administration.

To get a "good" job, you needed to pay bribes.

The fact that we were all fated for extermination didn't prevent people eager to make money from literally and mercilessly fleecing their companions in misfortune.

Unfortunately, Judases were, are, and will be among us.

The factory manufactured various trifles that were supposedly indispensable to the army.

Tin spoons, forks, horse combs, carbide lamp burners, air vents for bunkers.

Even when I was already in the Płaszów camp, I would join others to go and work in this factory.

We were escorted out and brought back to the camp (after twelve hours of work) by Ukrainian soldiers (collaborators of General Vlasov's army),[41] enlisted in the German army as an auxiliary service.

Perhaps you remember: they were troops in black uniforms who carried out all the Germans' orders, including shooting at people.

I'd left jewelry and what could be thought of as all our belongings with very respectable Poles, the Gryglewskis.

Gryglewski was a plumber (a senior member of the guild) whose business was on Garbarska Street in Kraków.

---

41 The Russian Liberation Army was a collaborationist armed formation officially created on 27 December 1942 from Soviet prisoners of war, under the command of General Andrey Vlasov. Its units were not used in the camps. The Ukrainians employed for "wet work" in Płaszów were not connected with the ROA, but were individually recruited by the SS, including from the POW camp in Trawniki, into units described as "volunteers" (SS-Hilfswillige).

He was also the owner of two buildings on Długa Street. Both Gryglewskis are now deceased.

At the beginning of the Occupation, when Jews were still allowed to walk freely in the city, I was registered with him as a manual laborer.

Furthermore, I reimbursed him for the tax he'd paid on my salary (I didn't receive any of it), as well as his Social Security taxes.

At that time, I'd already begun seriously looking for safe places for Annette, Mom, and you.

Annette even spent about twelve days with the Wilks, but she eventually returned to the ghetto.

For one thing, she missed her boyfriend; and it also wasn't very safe at the Wilks'.

You know their apartment. It's a small room on Krowoderska Street. The entrance was reached directly using the staircase.

Besides, the Wilks socialized with gossips. Not entirely trustworthy people.

You probably remember that hiding a Jew was punishable by death, or, at best, by deportation to a concentration camp.

On October 28, 1942, a huge, bloody new "action" took place.

That was when several thousand people were taken away, including your mother and your grandmother—that is, my mother.

As usual, there was a list drawn up by the *Ordnungsdienste*, meaning a list of people to be rounded up in agreement with the quota set by the Gestapo.

Other people who weren't necessarily on the list were taken

on an ad hoc basis, because every *OD-Mann*[42] feared for his own skin and that of his relatives and didn't give a damn about whom he sent to extermination.

At six o'clock in the morning, the deputy chief of the *OD*, Kierner, came to our apartment and asked, "Hanna Przedborska?"

Annette understood immediately and slipped under the bed.

Her bed was against the wall, so that by slightly pulling the bed away from it with her hand, she made a gap to slip behind.

"And who are you?" he asked Mom.

"I'm the mother. My daughter's outside the ghetto."

"You're coming with me," he said.

I knew him personally and said to him, "Are you crazy? Why are you taking my wife?"

"Don't worry, she'll be back in half an hour. She's only going to the *Appellplatz*."

Mom merely put on her dress, certain she'd be back in a moment.

In such times of mad confusion, you lose your head. Your movements are uncoordinated as your thoughts race and you become completely stunned.

While he was searching the other rooms, Mom could have calmly escaped and hidden in the cellar, thus avoiding deportation.

OD-Mann Kierner, who took Mom away, survived the War and was hanged by the Polish authorities in 1946.

His trial took place in Kraków. I was there.

---

42 Member of the *Jüdischer Ordnungsdienst*.

I didn't testify for the prosecution. So many people incriminated him that my voice was completely superfluous.

At the same time as him, they hanged the (Jewish) doctor from the Płaszów camp, Dr. Gross, the one who'd put little crosses on his patients' files.

A cross meant a death sentence.

When the doctors under his orders refused to perform euthanasia, Dr. Gross himself administered an intravenous injection of carbolic acid. In five minutes, the patient would be dead.

At every hanging of the *Häftlinge*, Commandant Goeth[43] often treated himself to such a circus. Dr. Gross stood next to the gallows, dressed in a white coat, to pronounce the death.

For both, there was no other possible sentence than the death penalty.

While visiting our place, in addition to Mom, Kierner took our roommate, the father of little Stefan (Stefcio).

At that time, we were living in the ghetto on Lwowska Street.

We occupied a very large room, which housed two families—seven people, plus a stranger.

The room was divided in two by a curtain.

One half was occupied by the four of us— Mom, me, you, and Annette.

The other half belonged to Stefcio and his parents.

---

43 Amon Goeth (1908–1946), *SS-Hauptsturmfüher*, was known for his extraordinary sadism. Among other accomplishments was his commanding of the Płaszów concentration camp. Sentenced to death and hung in Kraków in 1946, he is one of the main characters in the Steven Spielberg film *Schindler's List* (1993) and is played by Ralph Fiennes.

In their room there was also a small corner separated off by a curtain where an old man with a dog slept.

In the other smaller room lived a German-Jewish woman with her two adult daughters.

With each "action" of deportation, the Germans reduced our "living space" by cramming us into increasingly narrow spots, and very often the beds took up the entire room.

As chaotic as the deportation and extermination generally were, the system of organized looting worked perfectly for the Germans.

As soon as people had left the apartments, trucks arrived and under the supervision of the SS, the *Baudienst* removed everything found there, leaving only the walls.

A few minutes after Stefcio's father was taken away, his wife said to me, "Take care of my child. I want to follow my husband."

To this day, I don't understand how this woman couldn't realize that, by doing this, she was ensuring her own doom.

After all, Stefcio was her (their) son, and he needed her more than her husband, whom nothing could now save.

As she left, all she added was, "I don't give a damn," and I felt like shouting, "For God's sake! You're abandoning a four-year-old child, leaving him to the mercy of fate, condemning him to ruin!" All she possessed was determination.

I took Stefcio to the Jewish hospital, which was run by the religious community and where many children had been placed.

I would learn later that they'd all been shot and thrown into the building's courtyard like a pile of potatoes.

May I remind you again that your mother and your grandmother (my mother) were taken on the same day.

During her stay in London in 1971, my Aunt Gusta told me that my mother swallowed poison while she was still in Kraków, on the square where they were rounded up.

I'd known nothing about it, but such an act is consistent with the strength of character and courage that my mother possessed.

If it's true, she did very well for herself. She avoided the transport and the atrocious sufferings of the gas chamber.

When the cars full of people left for the Kraków-Płaszów station, all of them were loaded into cattle cars, and I managed to leave the ghetto. By what miracle, I don't remember.

I ran to number 64 Dietla Street, the address of the Geodesy Institute. I knew an SS officer of Austrian origin there who had remained, despite everything, an honest man.

I removed the armband and entered his office, asking him, with tears in my eyes, to accompany me to the Płaszów station to get Mom out of the train.

He told me to call a horse-drawn cab, and we headed for the station.

Unfortunately, five minutes before our arrival, the entire transport had left for the Bełżec death camp.

Seeing my despair, he said, "Don't worry, you'll find your wife again."

"How?" I asked. "It's an extermination camp."

"You see," he replied, "I'm a practicing Catholic, and I believe that if you don't meet on Earth, you'll meet again in Heaven."

And while saying this, he pointed his finger upward.

I thanked him, while thinking to myself, "What an idiot. Why don't you go there. I'd rather stay on Earth."

I took him back to the office in the same cab and thanked him again, for he'd shown a maximum of goodwill.

I can't remember whether you were already outside the ghetto during this "action."

The first home I placed you with belonged to a lady I knew named Stenia Jeleń.

I'd agreed to pay her two thousand zlotys per month.

I took you to her place with two suitcases full of your things and paid her two thousand zlotys, and you stayed there.

After a week, she asked me to take you back because of this or that. To make a long story short, she was scared. She didn't return the money or your things.

A cheap swindler! She had a son your age, so she kept two suitcases of your things for her bastard.

I brought you back to the ghetto, since there was no other solution.

My brother Dudek, who'd die after the War in 1946, also worked for the *OD*.

I told him that you only had one shirt and one pair of underpants left.

Thanks to some warehouses full of children's clothes, the next day I obtained a lot of things for you.

Do you remember the Hoszowskis? When you were earning your baccalaureate in Katowice, you and Wanda[44] slept at their place for one night.

---

44 Ryszard Polanski's second wife.

During a party after the War at Cesia Hoszowska's in Bytom, I found myself face to face with the "honest" Mrs. Jeleń.

We were sitting opposite each other at the same table, never broaching the subject.

As if I were seeing her for the first time in my life.

You came back to me in the ghetto, but by then I'd already started preparing another hideout for you in the city.

I packed all our underwear, all my own clothes, Mom's things, and everything else I could. Several times a day, Henio Wilk and his wife Kazia passed the packages one by one through the barbed wire of the ghetto and brought them to their place.

I made it clear to them that everything, including the jewelry, should be monetized and that the money should be used for your subsistence.

I also gave them a note for Mr. and Mrs. Gryglewski so that they would hand over certain jewels to them if needed.

I also gave them a list of items deposited with the Gryglewskis.

I entrusted a pair of diamond earrings to the warehouseman of the Waks company, where I worked.

This man was named Kamiński, and I could trust him completely.

I met him after the War. I'll return to him later.

I will now give you an example of the dishonesty of a certain segment of society and explain how it manages to exploit the misfortune of others.

I was working as a locksmith. My foreman's name was Stańczyk.

Although I was much older than him, I addressed him as *sir*, and he used the informal *you* when speaking to me.

One day, he asked me if I had anything to sell. "Yes," I replied. "I do."

It wasn't as if I had any furs left. I'd already taken all of them—mine and your mother's two silver foxes—to the depot on order of the Germans.

I didn't want to risk hiding them, because it was punishable by death.

They threatened us with the death penalty for the slightest trifle. In many cases, they'd shoot someone to terrorize others.

I informed him I had a very beautiful coat that had belonged to my wife, part of an English outfit, as well as a long dress made in Paris from superb black silk velvet, worn only once.

I told him the story of that one time she'd worn it: it had been at a dance.

After her arrival in Poland, she'd wanted to have it altered for everyday use, but I'd resisted and said, "We'll dance again in our lifetime; it would be a pity to alter it."

Fate decided otherwise. We never danced again, and your mother was an excellent dancer.

So, I brought him these items, but I never saw any money.

He started with lies, claiming that nothing had been sold yet. Then he finally told me, "What do you need this money for, anyway? You're going to end up at the end of a rope!" And he started swinging and twirling in circles, imitating the corpse of a hanged man.

I saw this man more than once after the War.

Each time, he'd approach me as if nothing had happened. "How are you?" he'd say. "Very well, thank you," I'd reply.

If only he'd tried to apologize a little. One word would have sufficed. It never even crossed his mind.

All the Wilks did was place you with that caretaker. Nothing else.

They paid her very little. They resold our gold—and they drank the money.

You know that Henio was always drunk. Kazia liked to toss them back, too.

It was Kazia who was wearing Mom's lingerie, as well as all her dresses. When I came back after the War to live with them for a while, she still had a well-stocked closet.

Henio was walking around in my best clothes.

His brother was also wearing my things. The shoemaker (a real crook!) on Łobzowska Street where the drinking binges took place also wore them.

I had not a stitch to wear when I got back.

I wore the clothes of my host from Linz, which I'd paid for with bread and contraband alcohol, and a coat made from an American army blanket and dyed black.

My entire fortune consisted of a few rags looted in Germany and Austria.

The Wilks were friends. They could have at least said, "Listen, we still have some of your things, so take what you need." But no, not a word.

Tosia lent me an old jacket of Dudek's for the winter, which I returned to her later when I'd already started earning money.

The next hideout I found for you was with Marian. I don't know if you remember him.

He was a short *agar*[45] who was a hardware dealer or plumber

45 Cracovian slang for "hooligan."

by profession and lived on Krupnicza Street, on the ground floor.

I don't remember the number, but there was a wide wooden door and a large courtyard.

Marian was a rather unusual *kind*[46] for Kraków, a kind of guttersnipe, but also a very good guy by nature.

He liked you a lot, and when I met him after the War, he couldn't stop talking about you. He died a few years later.

Your next "den" was with that very caretaker, and you stayed with her the longest.

I don't remember her name. Nor do I have much to say about her.

At the beginning, when I was still working at Waks, she came to see me to complain about the Wilks.

That they weren't paying her enough, that they hadn't given her all the bedding and mattresses for you I'd entrusted with them.

After the War, she sued me for compensation.

I would have given her a few thousand zlotys anyway, but I wasn't earning enough yet.

The court awarded her a certain sum as compensation, but I don't remember the amount.

I paid it in installments.

You were always unruly, perhaps because you missed your family, but who can ask for logic from a nine-year-old?

Twice you returned to the ghetto, and twice you miraculously avoided death.

---

46 Translator's Note: *kind* (plural: *kinder*): German or Yiddish for "child."

Each time, you chose the wrong moment, returning a day or two before an "action."

Once you were with Stefcio (you reminded me of this during my last stay with you in California), and a guy from the *Baudienst* let you go when you told him you were hungry.

Among those who remained in the ghetto, no one came out alive.

They were all brutally murdered, and the massacre lasted several days, because they searched for people even in the cellars.

For several days, horse-drawn carts carried piles of corpses to the Płaszów camp.

Just as you sometimes see a dead horse that has fallen in the street loaded onto a cart with its hooves swinging off the edge, they carried off all these mercilessly murdered, massacred people in the same way.

They had dug a huge pit beforehand, where prisoners selected for the chore (namely, us) were to dump the corpses.

The inhabitants of the ghetto were divided into two categories.

Group A was destined for the Płaszów camp, while Group B remained in the ghetto until the end to be exterminated.

The entire operation took place in utter chaos, amidst the monstrous yells of the Germans and perfunctory executions for nothing.

Identity cards or work permits no longer counted.

People were driven like cattle, lined up four at a time a hundred times, totaling four hundred people.

I don't know how many they counted, but at a certain point, the commandant said, "That's enough."

And I found myself with those who were supposed to remain and be liquidated.

Thoughts galloped through my racing mind. "What about my child, God? My God, what will become of him?!"

At the same moment, the SS man who was counting cried out, "Three hundred ninety-nine! There's one missing!"

I leapt at top speed to join the group.

In an instant, the entire column started moving, and I with it.

On Limanowskiego Street, I noticed you, standing at the edge of the sidewalk.

For the second time, the ground gave way beneath my feet.

To get closer to the edge of the column, I moved gradually, one row after another as we walked.

At your place, in California, looking back, we argued about the order of my movements. I maintained that I moved backward toward the rear, but you were sure I moved forward.

One of us is certainly right. Be that as it may, I reached the edge and told you to go immediately to the Wilks.

What you did when all was said and done, whether you went back to them, only you know, not me.

That was my last contact with you until the end of the War.

Here's an interesting twist of fate: I lost my father in 1912, at the age of nine. You lost your mother in 1942, also at the age of nine.

I won't describe my life in the Mauthausen camp to you. I did so in detail in my seven-page letter of October 21, 1973.[47]

If you wish, you can add it to this account as a postscript.

---

47 See page 62.

I'll confine myself to telling how I avoided death—a bullet in the back of the neck—on three occasions at the Płaszów and Mauthausen camps.

We were leaving the Płaszów camp in two groups of one hundred and twenty people to work at the Waks factory.

One group worked during the day for twelve hours; the other at night, also for twelve hours. Each week, it changed. The night team worked during the day, and vice versa.

The *Kapo* for one group was Ignac Taubman, the cousin of Regina Horowitz (who was Rysiek's mother[48]), and for the other group, me.

By *Kapo*, I don't mean the murdering kind, just the person responsible for the entire group.

He was the person who assembled the group to leave the camp and to return to it.

He reported at the gate which group was leaving, which returning, and what the numbers were.

He also assigned people to the factory according to the demands of the foremen, who were Catholics.

A Jew couldn't be a foreman, but many knew much more than those who were foremen.

We were escorted both ways by a group of Ukrainian soldiers known as *vlassovtsy*, whose position in the German military formations I've already described.

One day, Ignac Taubman told me, "Mundziu! I'm coming

---

48 Ryszard (Richard) Horowitz, known to be the youngest survivor depicted in *Schindler's List*. His parents were Regina and Dolek (Dawid) Horowitz.

with your group as a regular *Häftling*. My group will be led by Janek Beck [a colleague from his group]."

When we arrived at the factory and the Ukrainians had gone back to the camp (they returned after twelve hours to pick us up), he said to me, "Mundziu, you know people in the area. Try to find a place for my son somewhere."

His son was about your age, maybe a year older or younger.

I asked, "For how long? How much can you pay? Where is the boy?"

"I'll pay whatever it takes," he replied. "It isn't for long. Don't worry, I'll take him back soon."

I wasn't suspicious at all.

I went through the fence surrounding our factory and found a hideout for his kid with some women who lived in shacks nearby.

After a while, thanks to my intervention with the *Wächter* (the guard), he went out.

The *Wächter* was a kind of doorman, a man of sixty to sixty-five, a Pole or a recently arrived *Volksdeutscher*.[49]

After a while, Ignac came back and said simply, "It's settled." That meant he was going to move his son from his old hideout to the new one, which had been arranged by me.

---

49 During the Occupation, the Germans introduced into Poland what was called the *Deutsche Volksliste (DVL)*, a nationwide German list. On that list were registered the people known as *Volksdeutsche*, classed in different categories according to their degree of "Germanness." These people benefited from privileges, such as better food rations or access to German educational institutions, but they were also bound by a duty of loyalty to the Reich.

Everything returned to normal. He took back his group, and I took back mine.

My group was jokingly called, "The best tinsmiths[50] of the lawyers."

Other than a dozen real craftsmen, it included Dr. Kaufman, Dr. Schlang, Dr. Katz, Dr. Horowitz (not Dolek), and Dr. Pischinger, an important wood exporter and the second-largest exporter of iron.

The last two were wealthy owners of several buildings.

None had ever held a hammer, and suddenly they were tinsmiths.

Imagine how the work went, and whether Hitler could win the War using a "rear guard" like that!

One day, Ignac started up again. "Mundziu, today you're going to go with my morning group, and Beck from my group will replace you in the night team."

"Tell me, Ignac, what trick are you pulling with that?" I asked.

He began swearing by all that's holy that it was only about his son, how he wanted someone to take him to Kraków, and that I was in a good situation to understand what it's like to have a child with strangers.

"Hide in the middle of the group," I told him, "because it's Zdrojewski at the gate today." Zdrojewski was Goeth's deputy.

---

50 Translator's Note: Strange as the "tinsmith's"craft may seem today, some tin objects were still being made or repaired by hand during the War. These included household items (pots, pans), lights such as lanterns and candlesticks, building materials, and such farm materials as buckets and funnels.

The group left, and I shouted how many we were while everyone stamped their feet as required as they passed through the gate. Everything was fine.

Around nine in the morning, Ignac said to me, "I'm going out. I have something to do."

"Where are you going?" I asked.

"I have to go into town. I'll be back in two hours. Don't worry."

"Listen, Ignac, stop your bullshit. You certainly know we bear collective responsibility for what any of us do."

"Don't worry. Replace me and act as the *Kapo* of my group until I get back."

"Thanks for the honor, Ignac, but I prefer my own. And besides, you know my group is doctors. Anyway, be careful and keep us in mind."

"Don't worry, Mundziu," he said and left.

It wasn't necessary to report it to the *Wächter*, because it was his group, and in any case, he was the top dog.

I was lucky that he left without my help—that is, with the *Wächter's* permission—and that I wasn't mixed up in it.

Two, three, four hours had passed since Ignac had left, and all sorts of ideas were already swirling in my head.

I called a few of the oldest and most trustworthy comrades, who knew nothing about all of this. "Listen, guys, here's what's happened," I told them.

A wind of panic blew through the factory, because the others understood from the looks on our faces that something was wrong; and even though they all swore later that they hadn't breathed a word to anyone, in a few moments everybody knew.

Around two o'clock in the afternoon, a motorcycle with

a sidecar entered the factory grounds, making a great deal of noise.

It was being driven by a Gestapo man. Another was sitting in the sidecar, and behind him was Ignac, sitting astride it.

At first, I thought the Gestapo had caught him in the street and brought him to the factory to be whipped or shot in our presence.

The SS and the Gestapo were in the habit of doing this to frighten the other prisoners and discourage any attempt at insubordination or escape.

All three jumped off the motorcycle. The Gestapo men were striking their boots with the black riding crops they held in their hands, and the terrible noise they made added to the atmosphere of terror.

They flung open the door of the factory floor where we were working.

"*Achtung!*" I shouted at the top of my lungs, and everybody stopped working and moving and stood at attention.

At that instant, the Gestapo man roared, "*Kapo!*" There was a deadly silence.

Another roar, even louder. "*Kapo!*" More silence.

After a moment, Ignac pointed his finger at me.

"*Komm her!*" ("Come here!") yelled the Gestapo man.

I approached and, pointing my finger at Ignac, said, "But he's the *Kapo*."

"Can it!" roared the Gestapo man, "and listen carefully to what I tell you. When you go back to the camp, say that Ignac Taubman left with us."

Deep down, I should have asked with whom, because his "with us" meant nothing, but I replied, "Yes, sir!"

But I already knew the mentality of these people, these supermen.

You must never ask anything, never say thank you, only reply, "*Befehl!*" ("Yes, sir!")

All three of them got on the motorcycle and left.

From that moment on, Ignac became a Gestapo informant.

On the floor of the factory—panic. All of them were running in every direction like headless chickens: what to do, what to do?

I went to the factory office and called Zdrojewski, the deputy commandant, at the camp.

I told him on the phone what had happened. "I'm coming right away." He hung up.

A quarter of an hour later, he arrived in the factory courtyard on horseback.

He flung open the door to the factory floor. I shouted "*Achtung!*" again and went over to him to recount everything.

"Out!" he snapped at me. I went out into the courtyard. Pacing back and forth, he ordered me to tell him what had happened.

I pursued him like a stubborn fart, repeating the same story over and over again.

At one point, he asked me how I knew it had been the Gestapo.

"But it's obvious, you can recognize them right away," I replied.

He told me to call the *Wächter*.

"Why did you let Taubman out?" he asked him.

"But he's a *Kapo*, and he told me he was going to buy something to eat in the shop next door."

"Fuck off, you idiot," he replied.

Then he turned to me. "Come with me upstairs to the telephone."

We walked into the office, he telephoned the Gestapo, and they began to argue.

Suddenly, he realized I was in the room and told me to leave.

I don't know anything about the rest of their telephone conversation.

He got on his horse and shouted, "Once you're back at the camp, report to me!"

Ignac settled in Kraków. He got his wife out of the Płaszów camp and took his son back from the woman with whom I'd placed him.

With his Gestapo collaborator card, he became untouchable to the SS.[51]

He squealed on people right and left. He was the terror of Jews armed with "Aryan papers."

He was so brazen and sure of himself that he returned to the camp on the Gestapo's orders.

In the camp, he had a mistress, a very pretty girl named Helena Weisman.

I don't know whether she worked for him (which would mean she was an informant), or whether Ignac merely visited her for his minor pleasures.

---

51 The Gestapo (*Geheime Staats-Polizei*), the political police force founded by Hermann Göring, and the SS (Schutzstaffel), which was devoted especially to the extermination of the Jews and was under the rule of Heinrich Himmler, were two independent groups of the Nazi regime, permanently in rivalry when it came to competence.

Zdrojewski found out and ordered Ivan, the Ukrainian executioner, to shoot the girl.

The order was carried out without batting an eye.

During his career in the camp, Ivan shot thousands.

Ignac Taubman knew everything about you. More than once, he came to see me saying, "I saw your son. He was playing with his friends on Sobieski Street, or on Piotr Michałowski Street."

One day, he came to the camp and said to me, "Don't worry, the little one is healthy. He's growing up and playing with his friends."

He caught me in a moment of weakness, meaning a moment of stupidity.

I said to him, "Listen, Ignac, I have a pair of diamond earrings placed with a warehouseman at Waks. Go get them and give them to the Wilks, at Krowoderska 50."

"Maybe they need money for my child, and maybe they need it for later, just in case. They need to figure out how to sell them for a high price."

"Think of it as done already, Mundziu! For you, I'd do anything—you know that. Give me a note for this Kamiński [the warehouseman]."

I wrote a few words for him, requesting that the earrings be handed over to the bearer of the note.

I knew very well that Ignac had become a collaborator and was responsible for the deaths of many people, but I'd never imagined he could behave like a complete scoundrel, even while knowing that it was about saving a child.

Or perhaps he thought I wouldn't survive the War and his crime would go to my grave with me.

Except for the fact that there would never have been a grave, just a handful of ashes.

In fact, if I hadn't survived the War, his little theft would never have been discovered and no one would have bothered him.

Ignac was identified by the Resistance as a Gestapo agent and sentenced to death.

He was shot in Plac Zgody but only received a minor leg wound.

The shooter fled without daring to fire another shot, even though he really should have finished off that weasel.

Ignac survived the War because he even duped the Gestapo; and before the War ended, he fled with his wife and son to Łódź.

Łódź was not part of the General Government,[52] but of the Reich. It was called Litzmannstadt.

It was named after General Litzmann, who had captured it during the First World War.

The Gestapo liquidated all of its collaborators before fleeing Poland.

Even Annette's father, who was an informant for the Gestapo in Vilnius, was shot when the Germans were leaving the city.

---

52 Translator's Note: The General Governorate for the Occupied Polish Region was a German zone of Occupation established after the invasion of Poland by the Nazis in 1939. During this time, Poland was divided into three zones: lands in the west that were occupied by the Nazis, lands in the east that were annexed by the Soviet Union, and the central region that comprised the General Governorate.

That's what they called "erasing the traces."

When I returned to Poland after the War ended, I found you on Dietla Street at Tosia's. After we'd sufficiently celebrated our reunion, I went to see the Wilks.

They both told me they hadn't received the earrings and that they'd recently run out of money to pay for your hiding place.

Well, sure—since they'd drunk it all, and money doesn't grow on trees.

I didn't really believe that they hadn't received them, but what could I do?

Despite my efforts, I couldn't find Kaminski's address.

He was no longer at Waks. None of the team that had worked there during the Occupation was left. Only unfamiliar faces.

But one day, while walking down the street, I ran into him.

He was very happy to see me alive, and I was just as happy to have run into him.

During the conversation, I said, "I still have a pair of earrings with you."

Without a word, he took the note I'd once given to Ignac out of his wallet.

"You see, I hoped you'd survive and come back to Kraków. So I kept the note, just in case, and as you can see, it served its purpose well."

I apologized profusely, returning the note, which he carefully put back into his wallet.

I now knew for certain that Ignac had stolen my earrings.

I knew nothing of his whereabouts, or even if he was still alive.

We eventually learned that he'd changed his name to Gołębiowski and had become the director of a textile factory in Łódź.

It had previously been a private factory, but after the Liberation, it was nationalized. "Mr. Gołębiowski" served as its director until he was arrested.

Doubtlessly, someone had recognized him and informed the authorities of his past.

Since his activities had taken place in the *voivodship*[53] of Kraków, he was subject to the jurisdiction of the local courts.

To this day, I can't explain why that thug, informant, and collaborator was ultimately acquitted.

Petersile[54] (you probably know him), a pre-war filmmaker who was tall and dark with the black mustache of a killer, was sentenced to five years in prison for participating in the making of a propaganda film made by the Germans and called *Heimkehr* (*The Return*, 1941).

He served every single day of his sentence. But nothing

---

53 Translator's Note: A *voivodship* is an administrative unit equivalent to a province in Poland and certain other Central and Eastern European countries.

54 Franciszek Petersile (1940–1982) was an actor and producer. For his collaboration with Nazi propagandists, he was in fact condemned in 1949 to five years of prison. The collaboration didn't save him from Auschwitz, where he was imprisoned in 1943, and from which he was able to escape in August 1944. After the War—before and after having served out his sentence—he worked in Polish film as, for example, a production manager, in the film *The Two Who Stole the Moon* (1962), with the twins Jarosław and Lech Kaczyński, who would become future political leaders in Poland.

similar happened to the actor who played the lead role in that film, Samborski,[55] who was nicknamed the Polish Jannings. He fled to the United States.

And Ignac is free! It's the end of the world!

And yet, Ignac, that is, Mr. Gołębiowski, was so cunning and clever that the next day, with his wife and son, he left Poland without any luggage at all—illegally crossing the border.

They were said to be living in Venezuela. Apparently, after a few years there, he was already rich.

The second time I avoided a bullet in the head from the executioner and murderer Zdrojewski was as follows:

One day, this wise guy *Wächter* came to the factory floor and said to me, "Kapo, I wanted to tell you something."

"Go on, speak."

"A few hours ago, a Jew came to me with a bucket, telling me he was going to fetch water, and he still hasn't come back."

I almost fainted.

"Are you crazy? Why did you let him go? Isn't there enough water on the site? How could you do such a thing? It's madness."

I called over four trusted guys from my group and told them what had happened.

"Guys, let's split up and search everywhere," I added. "We all have to be back in an hour. Not a minute more, and if anyone gets nabbed, say you're looking for a Jew who escaped."

---

55 Bogusław Samborski (1897–1971) was a popular Polish theater and film actor. It's likely he accepted the role to protect his wife, whose background was Jewish. In 1948, after being condemned in absentia by the Polish court, he in fact left for Argentina, not the U.S.

I said "Jew" as if we were Calvinists or Anabaptists—especially since more than one of us had Semitic "stigmata" on his face.

It was very possible he was hiding very close by, waiting for someone who was supposed to take him away.

And all of us looked like clowns, creatures who deserved pity and compassion.

As our camp had not yet received those familiar striped pajamas and we were traipsing around in civilian clothes, the commander Amon Goeth had a truly Machiavellian idea.

He had our clothes painted with yellow lacquer. Not paint, but a permanent, shiny varnish.

On the back, from the collar to the bottom of the jacket, was a stripe four inches wide.

On the front, over the chest, on the left and right sides, were two of the same strips, also four inches wide.

On the trousers, on the outside of each pants leg, there were yellow strips as well, four inches wide.

So as not to lose a day of work, the operation was carried out at night on the *Appellplatz*, under the spotlights.

We were entrusted to amateur painters. There were several buckets of varnish and several pseudo-painters.

Lined up in single file, we approached the bucket one by one to be varnished.

The varnish had to be applied in a thick layer, and often it soaked through to the other side of the fabric.

Looking at each other, we snorted with laughter. "What do you look like!" But none of us could see himself.

And it was in these circus outfits that we rushed off to search for the fugitive, with little hope of finding him.

Others looked at us as if we were crazy.

Generally, when we marched single file to work and back, the Poles would look up to the sky when they spotted us.

We returned empty-handed.

All that was left to do was to call Zdrojewski again to inform him of the situation.

Just as I was going to the office to call the camp, the *Wächter* waylaid me to say that a man was at the gate asking to see a Mr. X.

This "Mr. X" was the very same one who'd escaped and whom we'd been searching for in vain.

We ran to the gate immediately. At the sight of us, the man understood something was wrong and tried to run away. We wouldn't let him, of course.

We brought him back to the factory yard before conducting a thorough search of his pockets and clothing. He was a Hungarian Jew who either had the right to live in Kraków or was hiding there.

But that's a detail. What's important is that all his pockets were full of consular forms from various countries, and one entire pocket was full of stamps (just the rubber parts, without the wood).

He also had a small inkpad, for stamping the forms properly.

In short, a peripatetic consul for several countries, with his office in his pocket.

We arrested him, but to keep from ruining him, we immediately burned all the stuff found on him.

The guy who'd escaped was waiting for him to arrive, but his nerves had given way, and he'd fled earlier than planned.

The other had just come to deliver a "consular" document

from some country or other, with an exorbitant price as part of the bargain.

When I called Zdrojewski at the camp to tell him what had happened, he didn't answer.

He had probably slammed the receiver down, because as soon as our conversation ended, he was already in his car on site at the factory.

His usual SS riding crop in his right hand, he rushed like a madman to the door of the factory floor and roared like a lion, "*Kapo!*"

In an instant I was in front of him, standing at attention, chest out, trying to adopt the best military posture possible.

"*Komm heraus!*" ("Get out!") he yelled. I rushed into the yard.

As was his habit, Zdrojewski strode across the factory yard, constantly slapping his riding crop against the leg of his right boot.

I told him in a firm voice and in correct German how the *Wächter* had come to report to me that, a few hours ago, he'd let a Jew out with a bucket to fetch water.

How could he do such a thing! It was completely illogical, utterly stupid! He was an irresponsible man, and he was putting us all in danger!

As a finish, I put a cherry on top: "Fortunately, we've captured another Jew whom we're keeping in the room, guarded by two men so he doesn't escape."

"Who is it?"

"I don't know, but he came to the factory gate and asked to see the other one—the one who escaped."

First, Zdrojewski went to see the gatekeeper to give him a brutal telling-off.

If he didn't shoot him, it was because he was a *Volksdeutscher*.

I stood at a distance, careful not to approach.

When he yelled, "Come here!" I ran over to him, shouting, "*Befehl Herr Chef!*" ("Yes sir, chief!")

"Where is this man?" he asked. I led him to a room in the office where the offender was sitting on a chair, and where two guys were standing beside him.

Zdrojewski entered calmly and looked at the "patient"; at the same time, in a loud voice, I ordered my guys, "Back to work!"

They left the room. Now there were three of us. For a moment, there was a deathly silence.

I saw Zdrojewski wrestling with his thoughts and thinking about the situation.

What miracle kept him from immediately putting a bullet in the prisoner's head—not to mention mine!

For Zdrojewski, smoking a cigarette posed more problems than shooting ten people.

Sending people to their maker was a normal thing. His vocation. His hobby.

At one point, he said to the man, "*Komm*" ("Come"). They left the room and I followed.

They both got into the car.

Zdrojewski started it and yelled at me, "Report to my office when you bring your group back to camp."

"My God," I thought as I found myself face to face with him again, "this is the end for me."

SILHOUETTE OF *OBERSTURMFÜHRER* ZDROJEWSKI[56]

Tall, blue-eyed, blond, very handsome.

Before the War, Zdrojewski lived in Poznań.

He was part of what were called the "national minorities." Jews and Ukrainians also belonged to these categories.

He was descended from German settlers who lived in the voivodeship of Poznań.

He had studied in Poland and spoke Polish well, which he didn't admit since he felt so German in flesh and blood.

He belonged to the "fifth column"; in other words, a network of espionage and sabotage on Polish territory.

Zdrojewski was its main representative and leader of a specific territory, namely the entire region of Greater Poland (*Wielkopolska*).

At the beginning of the War, internal sabotage represented 90 percent of the cause of Poland's defeat and the victory of the *Blitzkrieg*.

You were only six years old at the start of the Second World War, but you probably remember that, for Poland, it was lost from the first hours.

The air force, railways, and means of communication were bombed so thoroughly that no command post could communicate with another, which caused indescribable chaos. Everyone fought as best they could.

---

56 Edmund Zdrojewski (1915–1948) was only a *Hauptscharführer* SS, a rank corresponding to a staff first sergeant in the U.S. Army. Goeth was a *Hauptsturmführer* SS, a rank corresponding to that of captain.

Immediately after the German army entered Poland, Zdrojewski put on the SS uniform.

He was immediately assigned to setting up concentration camps and co-opted by Goeth.

Since Goeth was of higher rank, he became the camp commandant and Zdrojewski his deputy.

He was a sadist and a murderer by birth and by passion.

I saw with my own eyes how Zdrojewski massacred the *Julag*[57] (an external unit of our camp)—three hundred and fifty young men—by shooting them in the back of the neck with an automatic pistol.

First, he ordered them to dig a huge hole, then told them to strip naked. They went down into the grave one by one, and he shot them in the back of the neck.

He stood in the grave alone, his cap pushed back on his head, smoking cigarette after cigarette, while another SS stood outside, constantly handing him a reloaded pistol when he'd emptied the previous.

And that was the guy who said to me, "Report to my office after you've brought your group back to camp." To this day, I still get chills just thinking about it.

There's one thing that still bothers me, but I've never broached the subject with the person in question.

When our walks outside the camp were over, on the hill of Płaszów, they'd created factories called "*Gemeinschaft*" (meaning "unit" or "entity"; there was one for locksmithing, one for tin-smithing, and one for sewing and lingerie-making, to

---

57 *Judenarbeitslager I* (a labor camp for Jews), destroyed on November 15, 1943.

name some). I worked as a simple laborer in the tin-smithing *Gemeinschaft*.

Although I don't remember why, I once went to the locksmiths where I came face to face with the man who'd taken a bucket to fetch water, forgetting to return, and in place of whom we'd caught that "pocket consul."

We stood for a moment looking at each other without a word.

It lasted at least two or three minutes. Finally, I left without a word.

I still wonder what should have been done with that one.

After all, he'd knowingly put me in mortal danger, and it was only by a miracle (even though I don't believe in miracles) that I escaped.

Beating the crap out of him wouldn't have solved the problem and could have started a fight with unpredictable consequences.

Denouncing him to the authorities would have condemned him to death, which is in neither my nature nor my character.

The question now became where and under what circumstances he'd been caught.

He certainly didn't reveal his name, nor the fact that he'd already escaped once, because he would have been shot on the spot.

Apparently, he had no other identification on him than a Semitic mug and a circumcised prick.

I also don't know what happened to the arrested man that Zdrojewski took away in the car to the camp.

When I brought the group back up the hill and entered the office, my legs were like jelly.

"Tell me once more how it happened," said Zdrojewski.

I began to run through the same thing again.

That the guard was irresponsible, that the whole team was trying to work diligently and obey the orders of its superiors.

And now, a bit of sweetener: we certainly did understand completely that we were only Jews.

"*Ja, ja!*" he replied, standing, and he began to pace the room.

It was never a good sign when he walked like that.

I could read on his face that he was wondering whether to put a bullet in my head. Or perhaps he was thinking, "In any case, he won't get away from me."

These were seconds, minutes perhaps—but for me, they were months! years!

I could hear my heart beating like a drum, like an African tom-tom.

And suddenly I heard, "*HAU AB!*" which means, "Get lost!" and I answered, "*Befehl!*" as I backed out toward the door without turning around, leaving the office like Napoleon's subordinates.

I was crying. Like a kid. The pain was tearing my chest apart. When I returned to the barracks, I was still weeping.

I lay down in my spot and fell into a leaden sleep.

The third and last misstep in my career as a *Kapo* was also my third confrontation with Zdrojewski.

A young man worked in our group.

I don't remember his name, and actually, I don't think I ever knew it.

Not a very interesting guy. Quiet, a bit sluggish.

He was distinguished mainly by a port-wine stain the size of a baby's hand on one side of his face.

Certainly, you've met people in your life with such an ugly birthmark on their face or neck.

Apparently, his parents owned a paper and stationery shop in Kraków on Długa Street.

They were sent to a death camp, and he remained alone. That's all I can say about him.

At six in the evening (it was twilight and already gray), the Ukrainians (*Vlasovtsy*) came to pick us up from the factory.

There were many of them this time, a lot more than usual.

They wore their black uniforms and carried rifles on their shoulders.

As I said before, they escorted us to and from the camp.

Suddenly, they scattered like a flock of pigeons, and only two were left to guard us.

I think that a group of Polish women waited for them every day outside the entrance gate to sell them vodka made from potatoes or beets.

They didn't have much cash, so they probably paid with various things looted from the Jews in the camp.

They grabbed as much as possible by looting those who were constantly brought from the city to be shot on *Chujowa Górka*[58] ("Prick Hill").

The condemned were ordered to undress, and even before the SS took care of their belongings, the Vlasovtsy had already pinched 90 percent of them.

I remember one time they brought an entire wedding party

58 *Chuj* means "prick" (slang for "penis"), but *chujowy* signifies "terrible" or "shitty." It's a coarse and sarcastic, untranslatable play on words that was all the rage among the prisoners.

to the square, with bride and groom, witnesses, guests, horses, and carts.

All of them, except the horses and carts, were massacred—doused with gasoline and burned.

We were lined up in fours in the yard and remained that way for several minutes.

The two Ukrainians left behind with us began to count us.

One was on one side, the other on the opposite, and a hand gesture indicated each little row of four.

"Four! eight! twelve! sixteen!" etc.

When they finished counting, and the count was correct, they'd exclaim, "It's correct! It's good! Fucking, yeah!"

"That's it, Petrov! Over here! No, over here, you son of a bitch!" they yelled at each other.

At that moment, the others returned in a large group, and the older one, who seemed to outrank them, ordered, "Come on, we'll count again!"

The two who'd just counted us a moment ago threw themselves at him, yelling, "Go fuck yourself, son of a bitch, we counted everything, it's good!"

And the other, without getting angry, replied very calmly, "Don't give a fuck, we're counting again."

He recounted the entire column himself—one was missing.

He counted again; there was still one missing.

"How did you count?"

"But we counted right!"

And they all recounted together. It was true, one was missing.

My deputy and I stepped out of the ranks and counted as well. And indeed, one was missing.

There was panic in the ranks, for obvious reasons.

A third one had escaped, whereas John, an SS man, had warned everybody that if one more person got away, they'd shoot fifty.

John was in charge of another section, fortunately not ours. The first time he shot ten. The second time he killed twenty, which was when he promised that the third time it would be fifty.

During the execution of those twenty, the following incident occurred:

The boy who'd escaped had a father, a brother, and a sister in the Płaszów camp.

When John was about to select twenty people to be shot, he'd first check whether the escapee had family in the camp.

That was how these three people were added to the seventeen who'd been chosen.

Seeing *Obersturmbannführer*[59] John, who was going to attend the execution personally, the escapee's sister, a well-built young girl, quickly stepped out of the line and, running toward him, asked in very correct German to be shot first, because the escapee was no brother to her and was nothing more than a common murderer.

He knew well he had an old father as well as a brother and a sister, and he had to be aware of what awaited them if he fled.

---

59 The military rank of *Obersturmbannführer* indicates a grade of Nazi officer responsible for commanding medium-sized units or specialized branches, particularly those in the police and security services. In this context, it's probably a joke.

Since he'd fled anyway, he was neither a brother nor a son, but a simple assassin.

"No, I'm not going to shoot you. Step aside," he said, ordering the Ukrainian to move her away.

The poor girl witnessed the entire execution, before being escorted to the barracks.

Go on and tell me whether it's still possible to remain a normal human being after such an occurrence?

Don't such experiences leave an indelible mark on a person's psyche?

To return to our counting, I shouted, "Who knows who is missing?"

And we immediately realized that the person who was no longer there was the guy with the stain on his face.

We searched for him for an hour, almost until nightfall, but the guy had melted into the background.

I explained to the *Vlasovtsy*, "After all, you counted us, and the count was correct, right?"

I also told them that the one who was missing was the one with the port wine stain on his face, and that his place was in the third row.

They confirmed to me that they had seen him, but "where the hell did he go?"

As I learned later, there was an empty tungsten carbide barrel around there.

He must have prepared this barrel in advance and turned it upside down.

I don't know how he managed to slip into it in front of everybody.

It occurred to no one while searching for him, to turn the barrel over. He would have been found immediately.

Apparently, the next day he was still in the vicinity, and he was shot.

As usual, after escorting the group to the camp, I had to report to Zdrojewski in his office.

My buddies said goodbye to me. More than one of them feared for himself in case Zdrojewski decided to use John's method (fifty for one).

When I spoke to them later, every single one of them hadn't stopped believing for a single second that this was the end for me.

When I told Zdrojewski everything, he flew into a rage!

I emphasized the fact that, instead of watching the prisoners, the *Vlasovtsy* had gone to buy hooch from the Polish women.

This time, when I handed over my group to the Ukrainians, the man who'd been missing was there right in the third row, and the count was correct.

The two who took control again divided us into small groups of four and confirmed it was good.

And it was while waiting for the other guards to finish their little hooch business that the man disappeared into thin air.

To exonerate myself as much as possible, I had to use all my strength to insist on the issue of the booze and the negligence of the Ukrainians.

Pacing like a caged lion, he immediately called the guard post.

After a while, the two *Vlasovtsy* who'd counted first and the older one who'd recounted appeared.

The two didn't speak a word of German. The third spoke broken German—Russian style. They told Zdrojewski everything and answered his questions, with the older one acting as translator.

Yes, they counted, and it was good! "Well yeah, it was *kharasho* (good)! Nothing to understand, damn it! I saw it with my own eyes! What a son of a bitch!" And they ended up arguing loudly.

I stayed there, as still as a rock. Like those stone monuments in Dr. Jordan's park[60] in Kraków.

I felt as if my legs had taken root, and each weighed a hundred pounds.

I must have been pale as a corpse, not a drop of blood showing under the skin.

I heard Zdrojewski order, "*Ruhe! Abtreten!*" ("Silence! Dismissed!")

He walked around the room two or three times; you could see he was boiling with annoyance.

At that instant, the office door opened and a German *Wachmann*, the guard at the camp entrance, came in. In one hand, he held a small pat of butter wrapped in parchment, and with the other he pushed a young Jewish man in front of him.

He reported to Zdrojewski that the Jew was part of a unit

60 Translator's Note: Henryk Jordan Park, built in 1889 in Kraków, was the first public playground in Europe. It was equipped with playground fixtures modeled after some in the U.S. Its creator, Dr. Henryk Jordan (1842–1907), was a Polish physician, philanthropist, and promoter of physical education.

that went every day to the Jewish cemetery in Kraków to take apart tombstones.

Upon their return to the *Lager* (the camp), he'd personally searched the entire group and found this pat of butter in this man's pocket.

"Okay, you can go," Zdrojewski said to the *Wachmann*.

"So, speak!" he asked the man, while dealing him two blows across the face with his riding crop.

"Hey, so you haven't got anything to say?" which was followed by two more blows of the crop, to his nose and eyes.

That was when the boy spoke in broken German that sounded more Jewish than German.

"Chief, I won't do it again, ever!"

All of it was in a pleading, pitiful tone. In a broken voice, exactly what you shouldn't do with the SS, and especially not with Zdrojewski.

He replied, "I'm more than certain it will be the last time," and applied two more fierce blows to the man's head.

"*Geh raus!*" ("Get out!") he yelled, pushing him toward the exit with the crop.

When they were outside, I heard two pistol shots, and Zdrojewski came back to the office while buttoning the holster to which he'd just returned his pistol.

Imagine my state of mind. There were big drops of sweat on my forehead and under my nose.

A monstrous pain was tearing at my temples. I felt and heard every beat of my heart.

One terrible thought crossed my mind. The next bullet was for me!

As he came into the office while fastening his holster,

he said, "*Du hast Schwein, dass der Kommandant nicht hier ist. Kannst gehen.*" Which means, "You're lucky the commandant isn't here. You can go."

Thanks to many examples, I'd always known that you should never thank the SS.

I simply said, "*Befehl!*" backed out toward the door, and left.

While walking the several hundred feet that separated me from my barracks, I wept like a baby, unable to calm down.

The boy, whom Zdrojewski murdered, saved my life.

At that specific moment, Zdrojewski absolutely had to put a bullet in somebody's head to assuage his passion, the impulse that compelled him to deal out death.

Just as a drug addict will slip behind a garage door to administer—even through his clothes—the dose of morphine that will bring him brief relief, at that precise moment, Zdrojewski had to kill someone.

May he rest in peace. Thirty-two years have passed since that moment.

Nothing remains of him, and I'm still dragging my carcass around.

* * *

When the War ended and the Americans gathered hundreds of thousands of German soldiers in prisoner-of-war camps, all the officers tore off their rank insignia.

In one of these camps, a commission searching for war criminals came across these two men, Commandant Goeth and his deputy Zdrojewski.

Since their crimes had been committed in Kraków and the

Kraków province, they were extradited to Poland to be tried in Kraków.

Their trial took place in 1945, or during the first quarter of 1946, and they were both hanged in St. Michael Prison.[61]

Hundreds of people who survived the camp and had the "chance" to encounter these men tried every method of getting into the courtroom.

I didn't even try. I had no desire to encounter Zdrojewski again, even though, in that situation, I wasn't in any danger.

But let's return to the camp. When I got back to the barracks, I was greeted by my unfortunate companions with spontaneous cheers, handshakes, and congratulations.

"Gentlemen, I'm going to ask to be transferred to another work detail," I said aloud.

This time, although completely exhausted, I didn't go to bed. I went to the *OD* (*Ordnungsdienst*) post and asked to be presented to the service commandant.

The commandant was a young shithead who'd let power go to his head. His name was Hilewicz.

His bitch of a wife, who was even worse, was the women's *OD* chief.

She wore a uniform like the German women, those high-top

61 Amon Goeth was tried on his own between August 17 and September 5, 1946, and hung on September 13 at the St. Michael prison on Montelupi Street in Kraków. He was the first Nazi criminal to be executed for his crimes, before those who were charged at Nuremberg. Zdrojewski was tried with eighteen others between January 8 and 18, 1948, and hung on October 30, 1948, in the same prison.

Lagerkommendant[62] boots, and a riding crop from which she was never separated.

It was said she slept with it.

I'd already been in Mauthausen for a long time when they were executed—by a bullet in the back of the neck, as a reward for having faithfully served the Thousand-Year Reich.

Hilewicz welcomed me with the words, "What do you want?"

I was at least fifteen years older than him, but he used the informal *you* with me, while I addressed him formally as "Mr. Director."

"I'm Dudek's brother (Dudek was an *OD* man too)."

"I know. So?" he replied.

"I'd like to be transferred to another work detail."

I told him everything, ending with, "The fourth time I might not be so lucky."

"So, what am I going to do with you?" he wondered.

"If I ask another *Kapo*, he'll give me a hard time, and I'll have to beg him. But if you give him an order, he'll have to obey."

That phrase worked. "Come," he said, and grabbed his crop.

Just as a marshal receives a baton on the day of his promotion and holds it in his hand during the ceremony, anyone with the slightest authority in the camp found it good form to carry a crop.

---

62 Translator's Note: A *Lagerkommendant* ("camp commander") was the chief commanding officer of a Nazi concentration camp. Holding the highest rank, he was responsible for most conditions and decisions.

He accompanied me to the locksmiths. The person in charge of the locksmiths was another *OD* man whose name was Ehrlich.

"Listen, he works for you from now on," he said to him. "He's Dudek's brother."

"I know. After all, I do know him."

I thanked Hilewicz, who left us.

"What barracks do you sleep in?" Ehrlich asked me.

I gave him the number, which I no longer remember today.

"Come tomorrow at one-thirty for roll call, you'll go with the afternoon teams."

We left the camp before two o'clock, which was the time when Zdrojewski received the reports presenting the head counts and the name of the work site, and he noticed me in the middle of a group other than the one I usually led.

"*Kapo, du bist hier?*" ("Kapo, you're here?"), he called out to me.

"*Jawohl Herr Chef!*" ("Yes, chief!"), I replied.

He gave me a kind of wink, or perhaps I just imagined it.

In any case, I was very lucky with Zdrojewski, who had a soft spot for me.

Perhaps it was because I "reasoned" quite correctly in German and explained, with firmness and precision, all the facts that had contributed to the escape of those three people.

But what did that mean to a man who had put a bullet in the back of the neck of thousands of people, cold-bloodedly and with a maximum of sadism? Doing the same to me would have meant nothing to him.

If Goeth had been in the camp at the time, I certainly wouldn't be writing these memoirs.

At that moment, I remembered something. Allow me to go back to 1940; that is, to our stay in Warsaw.

When they began building the so-called *Judenwohnviertel* or "Jewish residential quarter" in Warsaw, which they later surrounded with a wall and turned into a ghetto, at first you could walk around everywhere in that city, but afterward it was closed off without the slightest pretext.

All four of us left the unfinished building where Mother had settled with you and Annette after Kraków and moved to 40 Chłodna Street.

We shared that apartment with strangers.

One day, I left in the morning, to return around three or four o'clock.

At the corner of Żelazna and Chłodna streets, I noticed a group of Poles watching "something." I stopped and asked, "What happened?"

Noticing the band on my left arm, they replied, "Don't go there. Look. He's been there since morning, and he keeps hitting them mercilessly like that."

I looked too.

On the street corner stood an SS man, a strapping fellow. Every time he saw a Jew passing by, he ordered him over and dealt him a punch in the jaw.

The house at the intersection of two streets (they no longer exist today) had a kind of arcade, like galleries, to make navigating that street corner less dangerous.

I stayed like that for an hour watching that massacre, until I got tired of it.

I concocted a "philosophical" theory for myself: if I slipped behind his back, he wouldn't notice me.

Just when I thought I'd succeeded, I suddenly heard a lion's roar. "*Komm hier!*" ("Come here!")

No idea how that bastard noticed me. I retraced my steps and stood in front of him.

At the same moment, he applied a right hook to me worthy of a heavyweight champion, like Muhammad Ali.

It was like being wacked on the head with a club.

At first, I had the impression of something cracking in my head. I'm sure I lost consciousness for two or three seconds.

When I opened my eyes, my first reflex was to touch my head to check if it was still planted on my neck—or whether it had already come off.

I would have bet that he was a professional boxer who, for lack of training in the army, was using defenseless Jews for that purpose.

I went home, which was about 160 feet from the scene of the incident.

Seeing my face, which was apparently an ashen gray, your mother became frightened and asked me what had happened.

"An SS man hit me," I replied. I took two tablets and went to bed.

How long did I sleep? I have no idea. When I woke up and ran my hands over my face, then over my head, I could feel my hair falling out.

In the middle of my forehead, there was still a tuft of hair less than an inch wide; and higher up was a round bald spot the size of a pocket watch.

It was funny, but also tragic.

Black hairs were scattered all around, and right in the

middle of my forehead there was a circular hole that was bald to the bone.

I ran to a neighbor in the same building, a certain Mr. Bentman (a Warsaw native by birth), to get the address of a dermatologist.

When he saw my head, he asked, "Who did this to you?"

I told him the whole story, but he didn't want to believe me.

"Maybe someone ran a razor over your skull, and you don't remember."

"I'm not completely crazy yet. I do have a hole in my head, but it doesn't grow any farther than the skull," I replied.

He gave me the address of a doctor who lived on the same street, but I had to pass by the famous corner of Żelazna Street, where that SS man trained on Jews for hours.

I peeked out at the street by opening the door a crack. There was no one there, which meant he had already done enough hitting for the day.

I went to see the doctor, whose name was Dr. Higier and who was a "neurologist and dermatologist."

This indicated he had two specialties. I rang the bell, and a woman opened the door.

Was it his daughter or his wife—certainly not a maid?

During the period in which the Nordic race came to be thought of as a cult, Jews were considered "subhuman" and weren't allowed to have servants.

In the hallway, she pointed to the right-hand door and said, "Please, come in."

I entered a dimly lit, very cluttered room. It was very large, and in one corner, there was a desk behind which sat a massive man, somewhat resembling Orson Welles.

He had bushy eyebrows and big paws, and he was humming an air from Halévy's *La Juive* with a bass voice, *in petto* but quite loudly, "*Rachel, quand du Seigneur la grâce tutélaire . . . j'avais à ton bonheur, etc.*" ("Rachel, when the Lord's protecting grace . . . To your happiness I had, etc.).

Without looking up at me, he suddenly asked, "So, what happened?"

"One of us two is crazy," I thought.

I told him that my hair had fallen out just like that, all of a sudden.

Without getting up, he asked me to approach, took a magnifying glass, made me tilt my head, and for a long time stared at the spot.

"Have you experienced some kind of nervous shock?" he asked.

I told him what had happened. "Well, there you are. Well, there you are. It's as simple as one and one make two, as two and two make four, as three and three make six, and so on.

I'm going to prescribe a little balm for you. You'll take a bit on a cotton ball three times a day and dab it. Don't rub hard, just dab.

Do you understand what *dabbing* means?"

"Yes, doctor, I understand," I replied.

"And your hair will grow back as it was before. Or rather, not as before, but as now."

"How much do I owe you, doctor?" I asked.

"You have too much money, is that it?" he answered.

"I don't have too much, unfortunately, but this is a doctor's visit."

"Don't worry," he said, "go home." And he didn't take a cent.

When I told my neighbor what he'd done, he said to me, "And you didn't know Dr. Higier was crazy? All of Warsaw does."

A short time after my visit to him, with punctual dabbing my hair grew back.

* * *

Let's return to Płaszów.

The camp commandant Amon Goeth, that paranoid psychopath, was the lord and master of eighteen thousand men and women. In accordance with the doctrine of *Reichsführer* Himmler, which directed that the Jewish people were to be eradicated, his behavior was to remain unpunished.

Unpunished, obviously, according to the legal principles of National Socialist Germany. The Bible and the inspiration for such conduct was Hitler's phrase, "The law is what is good for the German people."

Like many SS serving in the rear of the German army, Goeth had to maintain the impression of being indispensable to the entire "extermination machine," a pillar of the Nazi regime.

For the Gestapo itself, the camp remained "extraterritorial" and was considered the commandant's kingdom.

Inside the camp, Goeth had the prisoners build a luxurious palace for him, which he furnished with the finest furniture confiscated from the Jews.

In this palace, he organized nightly parties and invited the Gestapo high command, because he wanted, on the one hand, to maintain good "neighborly" relations with them and, on the other, to show off his accomplishments.

The guests were entertained all night by an orchestra (a trio) composed of the violinist Herman Rosner,[63] the accordionist Leopold Rosner[64] (Rysiek Horowitz's uncles), and the pianist Jerzy Gärtner, who under the name Jerzy Gert[65] was postwar director of the Polish radio orchestra in Kraków.

The musicians were dressed in tuxedos, kept in a special locker at Goeth's villa.

When they arrived, they put on their tuxedos, and when they left, they put back their everyday clothes—rags.

They could only play what the master of the house ordered, and, as a Viennese, the son of a bookseller, and a sheet music publisher, he was well-versed in music.

They played wildly—until they were told to stop, because they'd never have dared to stop of their own accord.

Subjected to this permanent psychosis of fear, they were barely capable of performing these pieces accurately.

When the master of the house was stinking drunk, he'd stand in front of the violinist and say in a loud voice, "*Du dreckiger Jude, du spielst ganz gut, aber trotzdem lege ich dich mal um,*" which meant, "You dirty Jew, you play pretty good; but one of these days, I'm still going to kill you."

---

63 Herman (Henryk) Rosner (1905–1995),

64 Leopold Rosner (1918–2008).

65 Jerzy Gert, whose real name was Ignacy Izaak Gärtner (1908–1968), was a Polish conductor and composer, student of Hanns Eisler, Alban Berg, and Arnold Schönberg. He was confined at Płaszów, Mauthausen, and finally Ebensee, from which he was set free. After the War, for a long time he was director of a number of music institutions in Kraków. All three men survived Goeth, as one can see. Gert died during the anti-Semitic campaign in Communist Poland.

A fine thought—eh?—for the "trio" entertaining these supermen, these future masters of the world.

One day, after a night of drinking, when the guests had dispersed, Goeth left the palace at six in the morning to head for the *Appellplatz*.

Columns of prisoners awaited him, lined up by the hundreds, twenty-five rows of four for each hundred.

The deputy commandant, SS Zdrojewski, was lining up these columns before sending them off to work.

When Goeth passed in front of the columns, everybody tried to adopt the obligatory posture, lifting their head straight and puffing out their chests.

It was like the kind of thing you see on television when a military parade welcomes a visitor from a foreign country, and a president or diplomat passes in front of the columns.

Suddenly, two shots were heard, and Goeth's words to the man he had just shot: "*Warum schaust du mir so blödsinnig in die Augen?*" which means, "Why are you looking into my eyes with such a stupid expression?" There was a deathly silence as everyone lowered their head.

A dozen seconds later, two new shots, and words spoken by the same man. "*Warum schaust du mir nicht in die Augen, was?*" which means: "Why aren't you looking into my eyes, huh?"

In this case, it was enough for him for someone to look at him or not look him in the eyes.

You paranoid! You murderer! Not only by birth, but for the pure pleasure of killing.

Goeth had a mistress. A young Italian woman, a very beautiful girl. Her name was Majola.

As she'd expressed a desire to ride a horse and had never done it before, she had to take riding lessons that Goeth couldn't give her, even though he rode well.

The girl's idea was to present herself later on horseback in Kraków ("capital" of the General Government), with her very handsome lover Goeth, who was 6 foot 3 inches tall.

I can't imagine that a sadist like Goeth could ever have felt any deep emotions for a woman; that as a lover he could have been full of kindness and tenderness.

For him, Majola was without a doubt only what a cow is to a bull.

He was a degenerate who was completely engrossed in his camp and the pleasure of sending a few people a day to the afterlife, and he certainly hadn't imagined giving riding lessons to a girl.

He ordered the commander of the *OD* (*Ordnungsdienst*) to look for a good rider among the *Häftlinge* of the camp and ended his order with the usual, "Find me one within the hour, or I'll have you hanged."

And they did manage to find a young Jew of twenty-eight, named Kornhauser, who was very handsome and had served in the cavalry as well as having done circus riding, which he moreover refused to admit.

Goeth had a very beautiful rider's uniform made for him with high-top boots and a jockey's cap. Every day before noon, Kornhauser would leave the camp with Majola.

The road led to the Błonia[66] in Kraków, then to the Wolski Forest. After a few hours, they'd return to the camp.

---

66 *Błonia*: A 119-acre park in Kraków, the location of the historic mass celebrated by Pope John Paul II in 1979.

Kornhauser had received orders from Goeth to always remain behind the amazon. But they themselves were the only ones who knew how they rode outside the camp.

Since he had to give her lessons, he couldn't talk to the back of her horse.

Nor could he tell Goeth about it. For him, there was only one answer: "Yes sir, Commandant."

One day, they inadvertently entered the camp through the main entrance gate, side by side.

Goeth probably noticed it from the windows of his palace, because it was located precisely opposite the main gate.

While Kornhauser jumped off his horse and held Majola's horse by the bridle so she could dismount, Goeth came out of his residence.

"*Na ja, schön, drehe dich um und lauf!*" he shouted, which means, "Well, well, turn around and take off!" And with a few bullets, he shot him dead on the spot.

* * *

One evening, he had ten competent female typists brought from the camp.

Out of the eighteen thousand people in the camp, at least 65 percent of whom were women, this wasn't very difficult.

When they were brought before the camp office, Goeth was standing in front of the door.

He greeted them with, "So you're the Jewish whores who claim to know how to write? Come on, Sarahs."

For him, every Jewish woman was a Sarah, and every Jewish man was a Solomon.

What these women typed during the night no one ever found out.

When they'd finished their work at five in the morning, Ivan and six Ukrainians were already waiting for them in front of the building.

They led all ten to Prick Hill and shot them.

* * *

Goeth constantly strove to expand, develop, and enlarge his camp, by constantly expelling the Poles from the surrounding area, from their cottages and adjacent properties.

They had a maximum of two hours to clear out, and they were allowed to take a bundle of belongings weighing 44 pounds at most.

Goeth's ambition was for Himmler to visit his camp, too.

Himmler visited several, quite often, but apparently he was afraid to be seen in the General Government.

Later, in Mauthausen, I had the pleasure of standing for hours on the *Appellplatz* with thirty thousand other inmates when this degenerate—the greatest murderer of all time—visited our camp.

To celebrate the event, we were served milk soup with dried plums (which were completely wormy with tiny white worms floating on the surface).

One time, large quantities of planks were delivered to the camp in trucks.

They were stored in the yard, whereas they could have been transported directly to their destination, where prisoners were constantly building new barracks.

But delivering the planks at this particular location wasn't decided arbitrarily.

It was needed to martyr two thousand women who had to spend twelve hours a day carrying these long planks (one on the back of their right shoulder and one on the front) to the construction site.

The two thousand women formed a gigantic circle.

They went down the left side of the meadow and came up the right side, so that the circle closed like a hoop.

This entire delirious dance was observed by a young SS man, who wasn't very interesting. He was twenty-five to twenty-eight years old, not very tall, and a bit red-faced. His name was Gross.

Unfortunately for him, his name resembled that of the chief Jewish doctor, who constantly stood under the gallows to announce the death of the hanged.[67]

Among the women carrying the planks was a young girl.

Seventeen, maybe eighteen years old and not pretty—but gorgeous!

She was petite and well-built, with a pair of beautiful black eyes like two diamonds.

I'm not at all surprised that she attracted the attention of SS Gross.

He didn't make her work. She stood next to him, and they flirted like crazy.

That situation lasted several days.

You could see in Gross's eyes and behavior that he was

67 See page 95.

increasingly smitten with his companion, to the point of forgetting that she was Jewish.

I don't know—and no one ever knew—who reported this to Goeth.

One day, he arrived on his white Arabian horse and stopped right in front of the ecstatic couple.

Gross saluted him. "*Heil Hitler!*" and stood at attention.

"What's this Sarah doing here?" asked Goeth.

"She's counting the planks," replied Gross, embarrassed.

"Yeah, well, she's counted enough. Kill her."

All that was left for the poor boy was to take out his pistol and kill the young girl.

The next day, Gross was no longer in the camp.

No one ever knew what became of him.

As an *OD-Mann*, Dudek was assigned thirty women in the camp for the *Säuberungskolonne*, or "cleaning column," more commonly called "sweepers."

He'd deployed these thirty women in different places in the camp to sweep, but after an hour not a single one was at her post.

One had gone to the barracks to wash her underpants, another had left to cook up some kind of gruel, while the third had simply gone to bed. All had left their brooms or shovels anywhere.

Dudek had to run all over the barracks looking for them. Often, he'd beat one of them with his *Reitpeitsche* (riding crop).

Without a doubt, more than once he happened to call them "dirty whores," and it's for that reason he was accused of sadism.

Unlike the accused, none of these women realized the gravity of their behavior, nor how blatantly they were putting everyone in mortal danger, and first and foremost the accused himself.

For Dudek's trial,[68] at the end of his plea, his lawyer, Dr. Aschenbrenner, brought up a situation similar to Dudek's, which befell another *OD-Mann*. The consequences were as follows:

This particular *OD-Mann* supervised a night team of locksmiths.

His staff numbered 105 people, who were supposed to be present in the workshop (the barracks) at all times. That was where they worked.

Anyone wanting to go to the latrines had to be entered in the register and also had to return five minutes later and report it.

At two o'clock in the morning, Commandant Goeth burst into the barracks.

He was coming back from what we called the "party"—quite drunk, to put it mildly.

He was swaying a little but was still on his feet.

After a binge, his innate sadism and criminal instincts usually doubled.

In such a state, he was capable of shooting half the camp.

The camp's size, that is, the number of prisoners, depended on the number of people killed in a given period.

He always went around accompanied by two enormous Great Danes of exceptional beauty.

They were taken care of—that is, kept clean—every day by a Jewish prisoner who also dished out the food prepared for them in the SS kitchen.

---

68 See page 57.

One day, Goeth saw through the window of his quarters that the girl who brought bowls of food for the dogs had taken and eaten a potato.

He ran out of the villa like a madman and ordered the dogs to tear her to pieces.

Although they'd been specially trained to tear people apart, the dogs gazed at him without understanding because they were used to this young girl taking care of them and feeding them.

That's why they didn't attack her, an insubordination that further excited the monster's fury.

And so, as usual, he killed her with two bullets in the back of the neck.

The dogs were named Ralf and Rolf. You weren't allowed to address them other than by the terms "Herr Ralf" and "Herr Rolf."

If any of the *Häftlinge* dared to call them by their name, without the "*Herr*," Goeth would order them to make mincemeat out of the offender.

And the dogs would carry out his orders eagerly.

When he entered the locksmiths' barracks, he immediately asked the *OD-Mann*, "How many men are there present?"

"One hundred five, Commandant."

"Fall in!"

They lined up in twos, and he counted. There were only 95.

"Where are the other ten?" he asked.

"At the latrines, apparently," replied the *OD-Mann*.

"Why didn't they sign in?"

Silence.

"Alright, we'll wait five minutes," declared Goeth.

When they didn't return after five minutes, he ordered the

dogs to tear the *OD-Mann* to pieces, and all of it was done in the presence of all the workers in the barracks.

Everyone had to stand at attention while the man being torn apart howled and screamed appallingly. No one in the ranks was allowed to flinch. Everyone had to stand at attention.

At one point, when the delinquent was no more than a pile of shredded, bloody flesh, Goeth called off the dogs, took out a pistol and, shooting him twice in the head, uttered his customary declaration: To paraphrase: "I graciously send you into eternity."[69]

Perhaps he thought that uttering these words would soothe his conscience, although he had no trace of one.

He uttered this "I-shoot-you-out-of-pity-to-shorten-your-suffering," several times a day.

The missing ten were sleeping peacefully in their barracks, without realizing that they'd directly contributed to a young man's death.

The next day, Goeth called Hilewicz, the chief of the *Ordnungsdienst*, and ordered him to deliver the absentees to him.

Attempting to save them, Hilewicz said—or rather, reported, since you didn't argue with Goeth—that he didn't have a list of them and couldn't go and call them up.

"Oh, don't have one, huh? And can't make them come? Then how about this: in half an hour, bring fifty people to Prick Hill. Ivan (the Vlasov man) and his company will already be waiting for you there. Otherwise, the first to be shot will be you."

---

69 Translator's Note: The literal meaning of this German phrase is, "I'll give you a mercy shot."

And so, without further thought, they rounded up fifty people, mostly elderly, whom Ivan and his comrades sent to the next world.

* * *

I saw Goeth only once more in my life, at Mauthausen camp in September 1944.

One morning, we were running to the quarry—we weren't allowed to walk there, only to run.

There were a total of four hundred prisoners in four columns of one hundred people each, surrounded by SS men holding whips, with German shepherds at their sides.

The whips were of the kind often seen in westerns.

Made of ash-colored leather, they were about 6 feet long, so that when a "patient" was struck on the back of the neck and the whip wrapped around it, the person holding the whip could easily pull him toward him and right to his knees.

A few feet from our columns stood Goeth.

When he saw us, he shouted, *"Dass sind ja meine Juden!"* that is, "But these are my Jews!"

In his mind, we were his property.

Goeth was without officer's insignia and without a belt.

In 1944, when the Russian front approached the city, the Kraków camp (meaning, the Płaszów camp) had been dismantled.

Once torn from his little "extraterritoriality," Goeth was targeted by the Gestapo, who had had their eye on him for a long time, and for good reason.

He was accused of having appropriated colossal quantities of gold and diamonds, looted from the Jews.

And the Jews had been brought to the Płaszów camp from all over the General Government.

Goeth also participated in many cities in the liquidation of Jewish ghettos.

He spent very little time behind bars.

I don't know how he got out of it, but he was demoted to the rank of private.

He'd come to Mauthausen because he thought he'd find a lucrative job there, but the ring of torturers there was smarter than him and kept him away from their feeding trough.

Before the liquidation of the Kraków (Płaszów) camp, they exterminated all the Jewish "heavies" who were in their service and had hoped to survive the War that way.

The *OD* commandant, Hilewicz, and his wife (a hateful bitch), who thought themselves "second only to God," were shot by Goeth with his own hands.

Before shooting them, he said to them in a mocking tone of voice, "I promised you so many times I'd shoot you that I can't leave you without keeping my word. What would you have thought of me?"

Afterward I spoke with people on several occasions who survived the War and who were on the last transport from Płaszów, and they confirmed the authenticity of these words.

* * *

I was next sent to the Mauthausen camp. I've already described life and work there in my letter of October 21, 1973.

I'll only recount one more case where a miracle saved me from a bullet in the back of the neck.

It was a beautiful sunny Sunday in September 1944.

We hadn't gone to work that day, and there were guys hanging around the barracks, as well as on a kind of thirteen-foot-wide concrete strip between barracks no. 22 and barracks no. 23.

At one point, our block chief called me. He was a Viennese and a professional criminal, with a "green triangle" tattooed on his face.[70] His name was Franzl. "*Komm mal hier, du Schwarzer*" ("Come over here, blackie.")

I approached him and took off my striped cap. "Yes, chief!"

"Park your ass over there at the corner of the block, and make damn sure not a single guy changes blocks. They can walk on the concrete, but under no circumstances can they move from one block to another."

"Yes, chief, yes sir!" I replied, and took my position at the corner.

I leaned against the barrack wall, and my thoughts took off for Kraków.

My God! My God! My son is over there, my child.

Is he still alive? But really, what do I have to do with this war? What do I care about it?

Why am I being kept here?

Have I ever harmed anyone?

I have to survive, to see Germany's shame!!!

---

70 Translator's Note: A green triangle was part of the Nazi insignia used in classifying prisoners and stood for "professional criminal." Of course, such imagery appeared on the prisoner's uniform, not face, and the idea is used here metaphorically.

When Germany loses this war (and it absolutely will), I don't think anyone will want to shake their hand for a century.

How wonderful it will be when all the nations of Europe force the Germans to rebuild everything they've destroyed.

A sharp slap tore me away from these fantastic reveries.

I looked up. Standing before me was a strapping SS man, his face ravaged by smallpox.

I hurriedly took off my magnificent striped cap and said, *"Verzeihen Sie, Herr Schef, ich habe nicht bemerkt!"* ("Forgive me, chief, I didn't notice!")

"I can see that," he replied. "What are you doing here?"

Small parenthesis. The camp's higher authorities always addressed me affectionately with *"du Scheisskübel verkommener,"* or *"du Drecksack,"* or *"du Arschloch"*[71] ("degenerate shit-bucket," "sack of shit," "asshole"); and here, suddenly, was this formal "you"? I was dumbfounded.

I replied that the block chief had ordered me to stand there and keep the *Häftlinge* from passing from one block to another.

"*Ach, so,*" he said, meaning "Ah, I see."

"So: what is your profession?"

"Locksmith-mechanic," I replied.

"Ah, I see! And for how long?" he asked.

"For sixteen years."

And now, the indispensable conclusion of his interrogation.

"Glauben Sie den Frieden zu erleben?" Namely: "Do you believe you will live to see peace?"

---

71 In German, the SS-man used a really formal "Sie."

In other words, "Do you believe you will see the end of the War?"

"No, I do not believe it!" I said.

"That's accurate," he replied, and he walked away.

I went to my block 22 and told Jurek about the incident, who exclaimed, "But you were lucky, my friend! Your presence of mind didn't betray you. He's already liquidated plenty of people that way. When someone answers that they hope to get out of the War alive, he tells them to turn around and puts a bullet in the back of their neck. You shut him up by telling him you weren't counting on it, and so he thought to himself, 'Then suffer a little longer,' so he answered you, '*Ja, das stimmt*'" ("Yes, that's accurate.")

Since I'm talking about Jurek: Jurek was at Mauthausen in block 22, with this Franzl from the *Stubendienst*, or "barracks service."

He was Cracovian, from Dębniki. His whole family had gone to Auschwitz.

All of them—his father, brother, and sister—perished. Only Jurek returned.

His mother and his children who were minors remained in Kraków. They're still alive.

I don't know if you remember being with me in 1945 at Jurek's wedding in that newly built church in Dębniki.

Immediately after the wedding, there was a reception, and when I refused to go, saying I had my son with me, Jurek replied, "Apart from my wife and mother, you're my closest person, because we survived the camp together. And that goes for your son, too, because he survived the War under different conditions, but they weren't much better than ours."

We stayed until the next morning, because he refused to let us leave.

The wedding took place in their own home in Dębniki, on Czarodziejska Street, not far from the Twardowski Rocks.[72]

I don't know if you remember a comical, yet rather unpleasant, incident that occurred on that occasion.

Around 10 o'clock in the evening, two couples excused themselves from the newlyweds, since they had a long way to go to get home.

Barely a half-hour later, they returned, and all the wedding guests let out an enormous roar of laughter.

It was a somewhat malicious laugh, but who could hold back in front of such a spectacle?

The ladies were missing dresses and shoes. All they were wearing were the kind of pink slips that were called "Milanaise."[73]

The men had neither suits, shirts, nor shoes.

Just long johns and socks on their feet. What had happened?

They'd been attacked by Russian soldiers (known as *Russkies*), who'd given them a choice.

Either they took everything off of their own free will, or they'd get a bullet in the head. After which, their clothes would be taken from them anyway.

It was the right choice. They were in their underwear, but they were alive.

---

72 Translator's Note: Twardowski Rocks Park was created from a former limestone quarry in Kraków and named after a legend about the alchemist Pan Twardowski claiming the rocks were formed after his laboratory exploded.

73 Translator's Note: A "Milanaise" undergarment is one made of silk with a strong, run-resistant warp knit.

During that period, every night the Kraków militia found two or three people shot dead in the *Planty*.[74]

Jurek and his wife lent the two survivors some clothes so they could dress somewhat decently, since no one had many clothes in those days.

They drank a few more vodkas, and before noon, we all left for the Dębniki bridge.

Allow me now to return to other facts concerning the camps. On May 5, 1945, echoes of cannon fire were already clearly reaching the camp, which meant the front was very close.

At six in the morning, we were all already on the *Appellplatz*.

That included all the SS, the entire staff of the watchtowers around the camp, and His Lordship the camp commandant himself, whose name was Schöpperle.

He was a gentleman with a university education, wearing civilian clothes. He was a musician, elegant and well-dressed, with the manners of a gentleman.

All these highfalutin qualities didn't prevent him from sentencing *Häftlinge* to death and hanging them for the slightest blunder.

We each received a loaf of bread and a pat of margarine—an extraordinary event.

We were told by the commandant that they were going to take us into the forest for our own good and for safety,

And in fact, we set off there with the entire company.

I had no idea what was happening, and even less that there was a trick hiding behind his concern for us.

The Russians, who tended to be more cunning than us and

74 *Planty*: a circular park surrounding the center of Kraków.

were skilled in guerrilla warfare, immediately grasped the situation and understood that the commandant's sudden tender words weren't sincere and were concealing something.

Our march toward the forest had nothing more to do with camp discipline, now. The command, "I want to see only one head!" was over. Now we were moving forward like a herd of sheep.

The *Russkies* called out to each other, "*Grisha! Petrov! Alexei! Michka! Ivan!*" *and* jabbered something at the top of their lungs.

It turned out they were exchanging instructions; and soon, surrounding every SS man armed with a rifle were three or four Russians.

When we got to the forest, we saw that there was already a deep pit in the ground.

I don't know if it was there naturally, or if the SS had dug a mass grave for us in advance.

The camp commandant suggested we jump into this "gallery," as he called the hole, for our safety.

At the same moment, the *Russkies* began to shout, "Guys, don't go in! Either it's mined underneath, or they're going to shoot us like rabbits!" And we all sat down together on the ground.

The SS surrounded us (in camp language, this is called a *Postenkette*, or "chain of encirclement"), and we remained sitting on the ground for several hours.

Among the SS, the superiors discussed the situation and apparently came to the conclusion they couldn't shoot us all, because there were too many of us, and some Russians were already becoming a bit aggressive.

When the sun had set, we were ordered to return to the camp.

But beforehand, one of his soldiers went to the camp by bicycle on the commandant's orders. He must have discovered that the Americans were already there, because when he got back, he reported "something" to the commandant.

On the way back, several SS men threw away their rifles and fled one by one, abandoning our column.

Either they had someone in the area with whom they could hide and get civilian clothes to avoid being caught by the Americans, who'd send them directly to a prisoner-of-war camp, or they considered flight the lesser evil. Better that than having to answer before a "tribunal" of the camp as the torturers of thousands of *Häftlinge*, who'd been beaten, murdered, and hanged.

The Russians immediately picked up the abandoned rifles, and suddenly—it lasted but a second—there was not a single SS man left with a rifle on his shoulder and the Russians had them all.

A real coup d'état lasting a few minutes!

And now the SS was no longer escorting us back to camp. It was the opposite.

When we got there, an American tank with a white five-pointed star was already parked in front of the entrance gate, and two soldiers were standing guard.[75]

---

75 On May 5, 1945, a detachment from the 41st Cavalry Reconnaissance Squadron of the 11th Armored Division of the Third Army of the United States entered the camp at Mauthausen. The reconnaissance group was led by staff sergeant Albert J. Kosiek.

The American officer rounded up the SS, with all the officers and His Excellency the commandant, and we ran through the camp.

God in heaven! It was pure joy!

Before going into the camp, I went up to the tank and kissed it. I put my arms around it and nestled against it.

Seeing the prisoners' euphoria and sticking to the principle of "I'd rather be a living bastard than a dead hero," which to me seemed logical, I didn't leave my barracks until the first frenzy—that first orgy of settling scores—had subsided.

Even though the War was over, several guys had been shot.

I saw their corpses on the ground near the barracks.

Several *Kapos*, who were themselves *Häftlinge* but who'd mistreated their colleagues by virtue of their function, and who also deserved nothing less, lay under the barracks, riddled with stab wounds.

They were covered with so many that they looked like colanders.

The out-of-control mob demolished the cigarette warehouse and stole tens of thousands of Czechoslovakian Zorka cigarettes, a few of which we'd received each week as a reward for our hard labor.

The next day, I saw the five bravest Russians, the real leaders, curled up in front of the barracks. Their bodies were black and blue.

Apparently, they'd found the jar of venomous snakes, preserved in alcohol.

They'd thrown out the snakes and had drunk the alcohol. Consequences as above.

What a shame for such dashing and combative boys on their first day of freedom.

In the camp, the Poles began preparing the red-and-white banner[76] and decided that in two days, we'd all go together to Linz.

Without waiting for anybody, I slipped out of the camp and took off.

I had no luggage. All I had was my striped pajamas—a pair of filthy, stinking, threadbare striped pajamas—a dirty shirt, old worn-out clogs without socks, a deep enameled wash bowl with a hole pierced on the side and a hook I made myself to be able to hang it off my backside, a zinc spoon—and hundreds of lice!

The lice would remain my intimate companions for quite a bit longer.

Leaving the camp, I decided not to eat too much at once, but to gradually get used to food, because, for the last five months, boiled potato peels had been the basis of my diet.

Linz was about nine miles away.

After so many years, how delightful it felt to walk freely, all alone, without spotting a single German in a military uniform.

The road was full of people! Thousands of *Häftlinge* of various nationalities.

All of them stealing, looting shops, especially looking for food.

During my solitary walk, I stumbled upon a smashed food kiosk, which had already been well explored by my predecessors.

I went inside and saw *a whole pot of mustard!*

Quickly I took out my spoon, scooped up a large portion of mustard, and put it in my mouth. Was that good!

I took another scoop—which wasn't so good anymore.

I took a third, but I was already starting to feel nauseous, so

76 Colors of the Polish flag.

I threw the contents of the spoon on the ground and put the spoon back in my pocket.

On the way to Linz, I came across another kiosk, also well looted, but I went in anyway.

Searching carefully, I found a bowl of pickles.

I ate two or three and felt nauseous again.

I took a large bowl of these pickles, and carried it by holding it in front of me.

I don't know how many miles I walked with this catch.

I kept switching hands, which wasn't easy—I wasn't very strong—until I emptied my bowl into the nearest sewer grate.

Thinking about it now as I write these memoirs, I come to the conclusion that we were so inebriated with freedom, dazzled by the fact of having survived this monstrous war, that our minds were incapable of thinking logically. Our actions had broken any connection with the good sense meant to correlate them.

Translated into your language: Dad kind of flipped his lid.

And here I was in Linz. Suddenly, I saw a group of people had come together—local inhabitants, Austrians—as well as my fellow sufferers who'd been freed from other camps.

They were storming a single-story building, climbing in through windows and doors—shouting and causing a tumult.

I entered too. And what did I see? It was a post office, and the invaders were robbing the warehouse of packages filled with merchandise.

Hundreds of packages lay on the floor.

They were cutting them open with knives, fighting over various objects—a real hell.

I was the first to find something: a dozen colored handkerchiefs. I hid them behind my shirt.

Then I found a pair of black tights, a pair of yellow shoes, a green linen cap, and a gray-and-navy-blue twill jacket.

In a corner of the warehouse, there was a pile of razor blades packed in flat boxes of one hundred pieces.

I took a whole pile of these boxes. I don't know how many anymore. In any case, it was as many as I could carry.

I went through the door and immediately threw away my old clothes and put on new ones.

I hadn't found a shirt or underwear, but I got rid of my old things and put tights and a jacket on my bare body.

Imagine now how magnificent your dad looked!

Black tights down to the ankles, but the cut was German, so they were a little baggy on the sides; yellow shoes with neither socks nor laces; a gray-and-navy-blue twill jacket; no shirt; and a green cap for my head.

Like students in Kraków during carnival.

However, I couldn't get rid of the lice; and after ten minutes, they started biting again.

I put the handkerchiefs in my trouser pockets, hung the basin behind me, and put the spoon in my jacket pocket, all while carrying the boxes of razor blades with both hands.

It weighed a ton, but in the end, what did I care?

I had literally nothing, absolutely nothing, except my body, my blood, my thirst for life, and my faithful little lice.

I dropped all my Gillette razors on the street corner and left with a light heart after getting rid of such a burden.

In Linz, the crowd of *Häftlinge* was made up of twenty-three different nationalities.

They were running all over the city. Sixty percent of its inhabitants had left before the arrival of the American troops.

These guys were looting everything they could get their hands on. They were cooking in the street, putting pots on bricks and lighting fires under them.

The contents of the pots varied. It was a large, multilingual, and cosmopolitan camp of "nomads."

I met two guys from Poland—from Kraków, like me—and I told them, "We need to find decent accommodations. We can't keep wandering around the streets like this. After all, almost all the inhabitants of Linz have left their homes and fled the city, and the Americans won't let thousands of thieves wander around looting."

A few days later, my words came true when trucks entered the city, and the whole herd was brought back to the camp.

They didn't harm them or make them work, and they fed them well; but they were prohibited from leaving the camp and wandering around the city.

A complete census was taken, and columns of vehicles and repatriation trains were sent as far as possible toward countries all over Europe.

As I mentioned earlier, we found a vacant three-room apartment in Linz.

On the first day, I began rummaging through everything and reading the owner's correspondence.

It turned out that his name was Tratning, that he was an engineer, and that during the Occupation, he'd lived in Kraków in the German neighborhood of Juliusz Leo Street (which was changed to Dzierżyński Street[77] during the Communist era).

---

77 In 1990, this street name was changed back to that of its original patron, Juliusz Franciszek Leo (1861–1918), a politician, economist, jurist, and mayor of Kraków between 1904 and 1918.

His activities in Kraków consisted of working for the Wehrmacht, but I couldn't determine in what capacity.

Apart from the furniture and appliances, there was nothing else in the apartment. The closets were empty. I myself still had no shirt or underwear and was dressed like a clown from the Medrano circus in Paris!

All that was left for me to do was to search through other apartments.

I finally found everything that I and my two companions needed.

I started changing my underwear every day and throwing them away immediately, until I got rid of the lice.

This was because the lice kept coming back, even if I washed myself thoroughly every day—I still don't know from where or how.

At the barber's, I had my head shaved completely, to make it easier to wash well every day.

I paid the hairdresser with a can of Nestlé's milk.

I'll explain. I visited all the cellars in Linz.

In one of them, I found a whole box containing sixty cans of Nestlé's condensed sweetened milk.

I lugged it to our apartment, for fear of it being "stolen"!

Right there on the spot, I swallowed half a can and, within a few hours, the rest of it.

The milk and sugar put me back on my feet, and the abscesses I had on the calves of both legs began to heal quickly.

My left hand was bandaged, because a small fragment from a bomb had injured it, and vitamin deficiency as well as infection of the wound risked gangrene.

I was treated in a hospital in Linz. I went every day to have the dressings changed.

The end of the War fell at a very good time for my left hand. If the fighting had lasted a few more days, it would certainly have been amputated.

In the cellars, I also found a dozen bottles of apple must,[78] a kind of apple juice, and brought them home as a kindly gesture.

In another cellar, I found a dozen crates of crystal packed in excelsior. Urgently, I dragged them up to the apartment.

I still had a few more pieces to bring up when somebody stole them from me (the nerve!).

With these crystals, I bought bread from the baker.

I had so many that I handed them out to others and sold some on the "stock exchange"—that is, on the black market.

In one of the apartments, I found a pair of suede Tyrolean trousers.

They were polished to a high shine, but shiny trousers like that were the peak of elegance.

They were trimmed with a green ribbon and had very pretty edelweiss embroidered on the sides.

In addition to all this, from an unknown owner I "borrowed" white stockings, Tyrolean suspenders, and a hat with various metal badges pinned to it and a feather at the back—what class!

I put on the entire outfit, and I looked like a real Tyrolean (or maybe "proud peacock" is a more accurate description).

While the survivors were still being rounded up in the street

---

78 Translator's Note: Apple must is fresh apple juice, often used to make hard cider and sold as is or fermented.

and piled into cars by the Americans, I stood there watching the show.

No one dared approach me, because I was, after all, a "Tyrolean."

One day, in Linz, while I was in line to buy sugar and bread, a little boy your age shouted, "Daddy!" It was as if lightning had struck me.

I cried like a baby, wondering, *Is my son still alive?*

Two weeks later, with the authorization of the American army (that is to say, the Sixth United States Army Group), we created a Polish center in Linz that began to issue identify cards.

It only took a short time to become friendly with the Americans.

I worked with a certain Genio Seidner from Mysłowice (near Katowice), who had lived in Kraków during the Occupation.

As delegates of the *Häftlinge*, we obtained the right to occupy Hermann Goering's hunting lodge, which was located in Leonding, about seven and a half miles from Linz.

Leonding is also the place where Hitler's parents' grave is located; his real name was Schicklgruber.[79]

The palace was a very beautiful building in the shape of a quadrangle.

A bit like the Wilanów Palace near Warsaw.

The paintings and valuables were gone.

They'd either been taken away and hidden in advance, or been looted by the local population.

---

79 Alois, Adolf's father, was the illegitimate son of Maria Anna Schicklgruber, and probably of Johann Georg Hiedler.

The most important thing was the great number of rooms, beds, bathrooms, and showers, as well as several kitchens.

The Americans gave us unlimited quantities of blankets and pillows, as well as DDT and the pumps needed to spray it.

Within a few days, all of us had gotten rid of the insects.

The Americans gave me a special card authorizing me to move around all areas occupied by the Sixth U.S. Army Group and to use all possible means of transportation.

On dates that had been agreed upon, a jeep with three Black soldiers would come to pick us up and we'd go to fetch provisions, which were supposed to last us three days.

These were "dry" provisions, meaning those found in UNRRA[80] packages.

Bread, fruit cakes, melba toast, canned butter, various jams in small tin cans, sugar, coffee (Nescafé), chocolate, cigarettes (Camel), and even toilet paper.

Let's go back for a moment to the apartment I was staying in that belonged to the engineer Tratning.

One day, a German man of about fifty-five arrived and introduced himself as the apartment's owner.

"Ok?" I asked him. "What do you want?"

"I want you to move out immediately," he replied.

"And I want you to leave immediately," I retorted. "I'll only move out to go back to Poland."

He didn't say a word and left the apartment.

---

80 UNRRA stands for The United Nations Relief and Rehabilitation Administration.

The next day, he arrived with an American soldier, and this bastard already had a kind of green armband on his left arm.

The soldier told me that I had to leave because I had no official allocation for this apartment. If I resisted, they'd be forced to evict me by force.

In short, he gently made me understand that it would be better for me to leave.

I'd already developed a friendship with an old Austrian woman in the same building but on the second floor. Her husband hadn't yet come back from the War.

Our agreement was that I'd provide her with provisions and she'd cook lunches for me and my young comrades, as well as for herself, of course.

After leaving engineer Tratning's apartment, the three of us slept in one of her rooms.

I transferred all my spoils of war to her place, namely the crystal and other supplies.

One day, her husband reappeared. He was a tall, elegant man, an attorney for a bank in Linz.

Our arrangement with his wife remained in force, with the only modifications being one more mouth to feed and their request to find another lodging for ourselves.

This last condition spurred our efforts to obtain Goering's palace in Leonding.

Almost every day I went back to the same pseudo-consular post as ours, but this one was Czechoslovakian. I'd inquire about viable rail connections because, in many places, the tracks were literally as twisted as mattress springs.

All of Germany had been so destroyed by American bombs

that—despite all the barbarity that implies—we were deeply satisfied.

In a short time, all connections and, generally, the entire railway network were restored piece by piece on makeshift, rather fragile ties. You traveled on them at the mercy of luck.

Often, trains remained at a station or in the open countryside for hours, because they lacked coal.

In such cases, the engineer would unhitch the locomotive, leave the entire train in the middle of a field, and go in search of coal.

He'd return a few hours later, or the next day.

A Czech friend told me that he'd already been to Prague and that the journey could be made, sometimes with passenger trains and other times with freight or flatcars.

The length of the journey remained the great unknown. There was no way to tell how many hours it would take, but you could get there. And you didn't need a ticket!

The next day, I packed a towel and my shaving kit and left for Kraków.

I no longer remember how long the journey was, nor the exact conditions under which it took place.

The only thing I do remember—and this fact especially remains etched in my memory—is that for part of the journey, I traveled with several others who were all strangers on a very dirty flatcar.

I don't know why it was called a *lora*.[81]

---

81 Probably because in English, a *lorry* is a kind of truck.

It was already May, yet the nights were cold. You can imagine the draft caused by being out in the open on a moving flatcar.

I was afraid of falling off when the shock absorbers slammed together, so I slept on my stomach, my hands crossed under my chin as a kind of pillow.

Another episode from my stay in Linz came to mind as I was writing this. I need to go back to it to ensure that my memories are complete.

Although my host had an Austrian passport, he was a typical Kraut.

Tall and self-assured. Even losing a war hadn't deprived his arrogance of a single moment.

At home, he was perpetually yelling at his wife. "*Bin ich der Herr zu Hause, oder nicht?*" which meant, "Am I the master of my own house, or not?"

On the other hand, he had the appetite of three people. One day, he said to me, "We need to get hold of a large supply of meat. There are abandoned cars in perfect condition everywhere. You're on good terms with the Americans. Scrounge up two cans of gas for us, and we'll go buy some."

He didn't mention money at all, because it was well understood that I was to pay for everything.

"Gasoline is a minor detail," I said, "but I don't know how to drive. Do you?"

"Me neither," he replied.

So I asked my friends, "Which one of you knows how to drive?" None of them did.

"But I will," one of them replied.

Well, if he's the one taking the wheel, God help us . . . We got into the car. The pseudo-driver was behind the wheel, the Kraut next to him, and I was in the back seat.

The engine bolted forward, and "*Gaïda, troïka!*"[82] off we went like emperors.

About twenty-five or thirty miles from Linz, we bought a large chunk of horsemeat from the butcher.

It must have been a big animal. We had a great deal of trouble loading our prize into the car.

While pushing, I glanced at the shops around and noticed a sign that said, "Bakery."

I went in, told the owner that I was a camp survivor, and asked her to sell us bread for me and my friends.

She sold me eight round loaves.

I loaded the bread into the car, and we set off back to Linz.

As our "driver" wasn't going very fast, and the curfew had gone into effect at 9 p.m., an American soldier stopped us in front of a building at the entrance to the city.

"Where are you coming from? Where are you going? What do you have there? Identification!"

At the same moment, an American officer appeared. Without hesitating, this one said, "Hold them until morning, and check where that merchandise came from!"

They parked the car in front of the building and locked it, and we were taken to a very large room (it was literally immense).

It turned out that we were in a school where the American army was quartered. The room in question was a gymnasium.

---

82 "Go, Troïka" is a Russian song with words and music by Mikhaïl Steinberg (1867–?).

All that was possible to do now was to lie down on the floor and sleep until morning.

I must confess to you that I slept better on that floor than I do in my bed today, and I was as old as you are today.

In the morning, two officers (one non-commissioned) came to get us and take us to the canteen.

We were each given a bowl of black coffee, an unlimited amount of white bread, marmalade, and a glass of orange juice.

The officer sent the others home and said to me, "You come with me. We're going to find out where this bread came from."

The horsemeat didn't interest them at all.

They just wanted to know if the bread had been bought or stolen.

My two companions—or, to put it mildly, those two big bastards who couldn't have cared less about seeing me detained—got into the car and took off like lightning!

Why was it me, *ausgerechnet*,[83] whom they detained, and not the German or the other?

And what if this bread really had been pinched? As sure as two and two make four, I'd be sentenced, and no one would care.

A driver, the non-commissioned officer, and I got into the American jeep.

On the way, the non-com turned out to be a very likable man; we talked the entire way.

He'd studied in Paris, was a journalist by profession, and spoke both French and German well.

As we drove for quite a long time, he became surprised

---

83 German for "precisely."

that we were willing to travel so many miles for horsemeat and bread.

When we entered the bakery, the German woman who'd sold me the bread looked very frightened.

I immediately said to her, "Don't be afraid, you're not in danger. The Americans just want to know whether we stole this bread or you sold it to me yesterday."

"But no!" she replied, "I sold the bread to this gentleman, and he paid me for it."

"That's very kind of you, Ma'am. Let's go," he said in English, and we left the shop.

He drove me back to the school building and said, "Bye, bye," also in English.

It was on this rather unpleasant note that my efforts to feed my German host well came to an end.

I went to Prague, where I was immediately greeted by a representative of the refugee committee.

He quickly pinned a five-pointed red star[84] on the lapel of my jacket and gave me a card to collect one hundred Czech crowns and additional cards for lodging and "robes" (meaning clothing), as well as vouchers for the canteen.

At the station, when I grasped what was happening, I removed the star from my jacket and headed toward another exit, where the next delegate was waiting.

This time it was a woman from whom I obtained, a second time, the same allotment.

I stayed in Prague for two days. Not being able to be in two places at once, I had no use for the two lodgings. But I did

---

84 Prague was located in the Soviet zone.

collect one hundred crowns twice and took two sets of clothes. I should mention that they had entire warehouses full of this clothing.

As for food, I carefully consumed two breakfasts, two lunches, and two dinners.

My organism was starving after the camp. It needed not a double, but a triple, portion of food.

I remember especially enjoying the Czech national dish, *knedlíky*.[85]

After two days in Prague, I left for Kraków.

I was now richer by a bag of clothes and two five-pointed red stars.

This was the first small seed of my post-war fortune.

I arrived in Kraków not knowing who'd survived the War or who lived where.

I knew that before the War my brother Dudek had had a plumbing and bathroom appliance store at 20 Tomasza Street.

During the Occupation, this shop had been sequestered, and I would doubtlessly learn something there.

I put my bag on my back and went to Tomasza Street.

The shop actually was there, and inside it was my brother. Behind the counter was the chief salesman, aged twelve. He was my son Raymond,[86] or, as everyone called him at the time, Remo.

Our joy was immense, understandable.

---

85 Translator's Note: Czech bread dumplings.

86 Raymond was Roman Polanski's original first name. He also remembers this reunion very differently.

My brother was also full of joy, which I quickly spoiled with the bad news I brought him.

Six weeks before the end of the War, our brother Bernard (Benek) had been beaten to death (with a chair leg) by an enraged *Kapo*, a Pole. There were also some like that.

Everyone knew that Warsaw had been razed—on Hitler's orders.

So, after a week in Kraków, I went to see that city.

In the immediate aftermath of the War, as well as for months afterward, people traveled without paying. Anyone who felt like it could take the train.

Entire crowds of looters—why not simply call them thieves!—set off for the so-called "Recovered Territories,"[87] that is, Lower Silesia, and literally ransacked the apartments abandoned by the Germans.

The looting was total. After this frenzied mob left, only the walls remained.

They even took the toilet seats and toilet bowls. Doorknobs and window handles. What for? To do what? Total madness.

I arrived in Warsaw. I stopped on the rubble of Marszałkowska Street and cried my heart out. (Daddy crying, yet again—he had enough to keep him busy!)

I simply couldn't understand how they could raze a city that way.

---

87 The *Ziemie Odzyskane* were recovered or reconquered territories (covering an area of 101,000 km^2). The term indicated the territories to the west and north, awarded to Poland and conforming to the decisions of the Potsdam Conference, in exchange for territories to the east, annexed by the Soviet Union (178,000 km^2)

How much vandalism and savagery does it take to drive a man to destroy so utterly what generations have worked to build?

During my travels in Germany, I saw the city of Augsburg. There wasn't a single living being, except for a few stray cats. In that city, the houses were simply burned down.

Warsaw, on the other hand, was just one big pile of rubble.

I lived in Warsaw before the War. I met your mother and my first wife there. We left Warsaw for Paris.

That same evening, I went back to Kraków.

In September 1945, you were already going to school using all your strength to catch up on the delays caused by the Occupation.

Dudek was in prison, because of the unjustified resentment of a certain group of former women prisoners.

The shop was run by Dolek Horowitz and Tosia.

The house on Dietla Street where they lived was a veritable *kolkhoz*.[88]

Marian Gryglewski and Ela, Marysia Liebling's sister, lived in one room.

In the other room, there were just beds.

On one slept Tosia and Roma, on the other Regina and Dolek.

On a sofa, Nuśka[89] and Rysiek. On the other sofa, you and me.

---

88 Translator's Note: A *kolkhoz* was a collective farm in the former Soviet Union on which farmers worked together and shared resources. It is being used metaphorically because of the number of people sharing that dwelling.

89 The name Bronisława (Niusia) Horowitz-Karakulska (born 1932) also appears on *Schindler's List*.

I had no job for the moment. We can't even talk about earning money, because I hadn't made a single cent.

I went into debt at Tosia's, which I repaid as soon as I'd earned a few pennies.

Both of us ate at Tosia's for a long time, and it was Regina Horowitz who did the cooking.

Dudek remained in pre-trial detention for ten months, before being cleared of all charges and released.

He was defended by one of Kraków's best lawyers, a specialist in criminal cases named Dr. Aschenbrenner.

In Poland he had a great reputation for law and jurisprudence.

To properly characterize the permanent psychosis of fear that reigned in the camp because of its commandant, Amon Goeth, Aschenbrenner asked the presiding judge for permission to cite a few facts to illustrate the atmosphere of the camp.[90]

Dudek's trial took place before Goeth and Zdrojewski were extradited and handed over to the Kraków courts. If that had happened later, Dudek wouldn't have been tried at all.

In 1945, a few weeks after the end of the War, several liners arrived in port at Hamburg on orders from the King and Queen of Sweden.

These ships picked up several thousand War survivors who were convalescing in the former SS barracks at Bergen-Belsen.

During the War, these barracks served as recreation lodgings for sick SS men.

All these people left at the expense of the Swedish government, for what they were calling "recovery."

Not a single one of them returned to Poland.

---

90 See page 148.

Immediately after the War and the Occupation, people sought cheering up for the next few years and were more likely to try to drown their memories in vodka and by partying.

The nightclubs were downright besieged, and everywhere there were twice as many people as the venues could normally hold.

I had two buddies. One was named Kazio (I don't remember his last name). He now lives in Caracas, Venezuela, where he made a colossal fortune in a short time, something that wasn't that unusual in that early post-war period all over the world.

The other, Romek Fink, is somebody you know well. He knows you, too, but you won't remember him. He now lives in the Federal Republic, in Frankfurt am Main.

We would get drunk every evening at the *Feniks* restaurant, on the market square in Kraków.

A liter of vodka and three big beers. That was how we drank: a sip of vodka, a sip of beer. Without eating anything at all. The three of us were too poor to do otherwise.

The main attraction was dancing, and there were so many enthusiastic couples on the dance floor that you couldn't even dream of walking around.

When I'd get back home around one or two in the morning, I would lie down next to you on the sofa without turning on the bedroom light. It wasn't a comfortable double sofa, but a narrow little thing. You'd always wake up and say, "Papa, you stink of vodka!"

I'd quiet you by saying, "Sleep, sleep, Remo, you're dreaming."

July 1974–August 1975

My family: in the back, standing, my father and mother. In front of her, my sister Annette. On the far right, my grandmother. The third person from the left is my uncle Dawid (Dudek). My Aunt Teofila (Tosia) is in front of my father.

In this photo, far right, is my Uncle Bernard (Benek)—whom I loved a great deal! My Aunt Teofila (Tosia) is third from the right, my grandmother—the tiny one—followed by my mother in back and my father next to Uncle Stefan, who is in the center. On the left, the other members of the family: one of my great uncles in the uniform of a Polish officer (Woller was his family name). And finally, Dawid, or Dudek, as he was called—all the way at the front on the left.

Chronology

1936: The Polanski family decides to leave Paris to return to Warsaw, Poland.

September 1, 1939: Germany invades Poland.

September 3, 1939: Ryszard Polanski and his three brothers leave for the East.

September 6, 1939: The Nazis enter Kraków. The Jewish population is estimated at 60,000 people.

September 17, 1939: The Soviet Union invades Poland.

September 28, 1939: Surrender of Warsaw.

November 28, 1939: Jews are required to wear an armband with a Star of David.

1940: The Mauthausen camp, built in 1938, becomes a major camp in the Nazi concentration camp system. Prisoners, primarily required to work in the granite quarries, endure extremely harsh living conditions.

October 1940: Construction of the *Judenwohnviertel* in

Warsaw ("Jewish residential quarter"). The Polanski family leaves again for Kraków.

November 16, 1940: Inauguration of the *Judenwohnviertel*, the Warsaw Ghetto.

March 3, 1941: Creation of the Kraków Ghetto, in the Podgórze district.

March 1942: Beginning of deportations of Jews to the Bełżec extermination camp; then in May, to Auschwitz.

October 1942: Creation of the Płaszów camp on two Jewish cemeteries near Kraków. Originally a work camp, in 1943 it was transformed into a concentration camp under the supervision of the SS.

October 28, 1942: Roundup of many individuals from the Kraków ghetto. Roman's mother and grandmother are deported. His grandmother commits suicide immediately; his mother will die in Auschwitz.

March 13–14, 1943: Liquidation of the Kraków ghetto. The remaining population is deported to the camps—to Płaszów, among others.

1943–1944: Oskar Schindler draws up lists that save the lives of a large number of Jews. From Płaszów, he schedules transfers to Brünnlitz (Brněnec) in Czechoslovakia. He will eventually save 1,200 people.

April 19–May 16, 1943: Uprising and liquidation of the Warsaw ghetto.

Summer 1943: Roman Polanski leaves Kraków to take refuge in the village of Wysoka, with the Buchała family.

November 15, 1943: Liquidation of the *Judenarbeitslager* near Płaszów. Zdrojewski has 350 young Jews massacred.

September 1–October 2, 1944: Uprising in Warsaw.

Autumn 1944: Roman Polanski returns to Kraków.

End of 1944: Beginning of the dismantling of the camp at Płaszów. Prisoners are transported to other camps, especially Auschwitz-Birkenau.

January 18, 1945: The Red Army liberates Kraków.

May 5, 1945: Liberation of the camp at Mauthausen by the Americans. Ryszard Polanski is freed.

1946: *OD-Mann* Kierner, who had arrested Roman's mother, is hung.

August 27–September 5, 1946: Trial of Amon Goeth in Kraków. He would be hung on September 13.